MARCEL DUPRÉ
(1886-1971)

RECOLLECTIONS

Foreword by
OLIVIER MESSIAEN

Translated and Edited by
RALPH KNEEREAM

Belwin-Mills Publishing Corp.

25 Deshon Drive
Melville, N.Y. 11746

AP 385

Library of Congress Catalog Number: 75-29762

This English Language Edition Published by

BELWIN-MILLS PUBLISHING CORP.
MELVILLE, NEW YORK 11746

by Arrangement with the Copyright Owner

ÉDITIONS BORNEMANN
PARIS, FRANCE

Marcel Dupré

TABLE OF CONTENTS

TRANSLATOR'S NOTE

This book is a translation of *Marcel Dupré raconte . . .,* published by Éditions Bornemann, Paris. The original work was issued in February 1972, and the following translation is based upon this first edition.

The reader must not seek a formal account of Marcel Dupré's life in these pages; rather, Dupré sought only to present an assemblage, mostly chronological, of some favorite personal recollections.

Throughout, my primary goal was to fashion a clear and readable English translation. In trying to strike a just balance between readability and strict adherence to the original texts, I was compelled to take some minor liberties. Occasionally connectives and punctuation marks were added or removed, when dictated by reasons of sense or style. Periphrasis was used when the conciseness of the French text demanded fuller expression in English to convey precisely the author's intent. Certain foreign terms, titles, and expressions were left in the original, whether by virtue of their acceptance in contemporary English or because of their resistance to reasonable equivalents in English.

A secondary goal was to enlarge the original edition by providing more illustrations, and by adding the numerous appendices.

I wish to express my gratitude for the invaluable assistance I received from Madame J. Marcel Dupré. For the countless hours she devoted to this edition, and for her many important suggestions, I am indeed grateful. I wish to thank Monsieur Pierre Lafond, to whom this book is dedicated, for his help. I am indebted to Monsieur Olivier Messiaen, who consented to write a foreword for this edition. I thank Monsieur Emmanuel Bondeville for allowing certain revisions in his foreword to the original edition. I wish to thank Madame Georges Humbrecht, a member of L'Association des Amis de l'Art de Marcel Dupré, for calling to my attention several important photographs, and Mr. Donald Hall, of the New York Public Library, for verifying record information in Appendix E. Finally, I owe a debt of gratitude to Mr. John Rodgers for his editorial assistance, and to colleagues, friends, and my mother, Sarah Lucia Kneeream, without whose encouragement this project might never have been completed.

Ralph Kneeream

Blair Academy
Blairstown, New Jersey

FOREWORD TO THE
AMERICAN EDITION*

Of Marcel Dupré's personal recollections, all his pupils were familiar with at least two or three; related genially, informally, in the course of a conversation, after his class. Yet they were never the same ones (our dear maître did not repeat himself), and none of us would have been able to assemble them, one after the other, as Marcel Dupré himself does in this book. And so it was deeply moving for me personally, to have read and reread these pages. The photos, admirably selected, which illustrate the text, further intensified my feelings. Photos of the organs Marcel Dupré loved, played; photos of the virtuosos and composers that he met in the course of his prodigious career; photos of himself finally, at various stages in his life . . .

There are at least four of these photos which particularly struck me. The one which resembles most the Marcel Dupré I knew at the time I joined his course for beginning organists at his home in Meudon and afterward his organ class at the Paris Conservatoire is the one where we see him, still young, with a very large hat and a furcollared topcoat. It seems as if he were about to speak, saying to us once again, as was his custom, "Look here, my dear boy . . ."

The second is the one where he chats affectionately with his wife, Madame Jeanne Dupré, who was the guardian angel of his career, of his concerts, of his entire life. Both of them are in formal attire, he in the garb of the Académie. I, as a fellow-member of the Académie, remember him in this distinctive dress.

The third photo is especially dear to me. Indeed, as an advocate of *son-couleur* rapports, I have always been interested in theatrical settings, in their range of colors and lighting effects that I wished to wed with music; and during my childhood I made stage sets, and I even performed all the plays of Shakespeare (the only actor

Translated by the editor.

viii

for a sole spectator — my brother). Thus it delights me to see the great Marcel Dupré deftly assembling a miniature set of a medieval castle.

The fourth photo is one of splendor. There we see Marcel Dupré at the console of the huge Grand Court Organ in the John Wanamaker Store in Philadelphia. Huge — this is to say too little — giant, colossal, immense instrument, with its six keyboards and its 451 stops. When I was very young, I witnessed the first tour de force of Marcel Dupré — the performance from memory, with a virtuosity never equaled, of the complete organ works of Johann Sebastian Bach. He was able to achieve this feat on the tiny organ at the Paris Conservatoire, an instrument totally unsuited for such an immense undertaking. (Fortunately, it has been rebuilt since! Happily also, the same series was repeated the following year by Dupré on the fine organ at the Trocadéro.) In contrast, the Wanamaker organ was suitable, and was perhaps the best for the vast stature of our musician's mighty "frescos." It was this organ, in any case, which played a paramount role in the creation of his *Symphonie-Passion,* one of the masterpieces of organ music. The staccato chords in *paión* and *epitrite** in "The World Awaiting the Saviour;" the light of the star, the oboe solo impregnated with Hindu modes, the marches of the shepherds and the Magi, and the exquisite prayer of the angels evoked by 'Adeste fidelis' in the "Nativity;" the suffering, horribly pulsating, and the bleak frozen image of the sorrowful Mother portrayed in the "Crucifixion;" the marvelous use of the organ reeds in the chromatic counterpoint, the constantly amassing brightness and great bursts of sound in the "Resurrection" — all this was and is magnificent, at Saint-Sulpice, at Notre-Dame, at the Trocadéro, and upon many other fine instruments (I myself have often played it on the very fine organ at La Trinité in Paris), but I am certain that when played on the six-manual Wanamaker organ, and by Marcel Dupré himself, it was the grandest, the most sublime, the most powerful.

I have spoken at great length of the photos. They do much for the book. Yet, to be sure, they would be nothing without the text.

Greek terms used by Messiaen to describe the rhythmic and intervalic structure of this movement.

It is necessary to read the text which follows with care, with respect, for it contains an entire era and, above all, an entire life: the life of a very great composer, of a very great improvisor, of a very great teacher, of one who brought new life to organ composition, of the greatest organ virtuoso who has ever existed — of Marcel Dupré.

Now he has departed — as one sees him leaving Saint-Sulpice in the last photo in the book. But his works remain, all his magnificent works, with a compact, yet thorough *Treatise on Improvisation*, and these personal recollections which will never die.

In my library, which has nearly five thousand books, *Recollections* by Marcel Dupré will hold a place of honor; it will be among those cherished volumes that one opens often, perhaps even several times each day, to gain from it courage and to find in it wisdom.

Olivier Messiaen

FOREWORD TO THE FRENCH EDITION

Marcel Dupré recounts some memorable moments in his life. In this text we find that simple, natural manner which characterized him at every turn.

Here we follow the prodigious career of one who became organist of Saint-Vivien in Rouen at the age of twelve, after a childhood marked by the rarest gifts. We get a view of those wonderful moments during the concerts devoted to the performance of the complete organ works of Johann Sebastian Bach, played from memory in a series of ten recitals at the Trocadéro. (I can still remember another of his feats in the same hall: an improvisation upon an original theme of Alfred Bruneau, which offered, in lightning succession, an allegro, an andante, a scherzo, a fugue, and a toccata, leaving breathless all the leading organists present.)

We read about the first improvisation in public of an organ symphony, played on the organ in the New York Wanamaker store. This achievement established Dupré as the greatest improvisor of his time, and launched an international career which spanned a half a century.

Anecdotes abound, thanks to his associations with Saint-Saëns, Massenet, Fauré, Ravel, Busoni, Rachmaninoff, Glazunoff, Albert Schweitzer; and unexpected incidents are not lacking, with American journalists, in one instance, or with a curious organ he played in Wales.

Because of Marcel Dupré's compositions, the art of organ playing was enriched. His improvisations were equally remarkable. All who heard them hear them still. And the most wonderful tribute is found in this question asked by Widor of Vierne when the former entrusted the organ at Saint-Sulpice to Marcel Dupré for the first time, "Are you sure he improvised? It seemed written."

A simple, natural style is not the only dominant characteristic of these pages. The warmth and affection Marcel Dupré had for his friends, his pupils, is reflected in each phrase, recreating that enriching and harmonious atmosphere surrounding a life which never faltered in its devotion to Beauty.

Emmanuel Bondeville,
Secrétaire Perpétuel,
Académie des Beaux-Arts

LIST OF ILLUSTRATIONS

AUTHOR'S PREFACE

I have always loved to reminisce with friends, to speak of unforgettable events and experiences in my life brought to mind, at random, by the course of the conversation. But I never had the desire to write them down. Thus, for many years, I turned a deaf ear to sincere requests, to the "you should write your memoirs," so often heard in France, abroad, especially in America. And then, on the occasion of my eighty-fourth birthday, letters came from all quarters — without a doubt because I neared the end of my journey — such a flood of them, so pressing, so touching, that I finally yielded.

I shall therefore try to bring together, across a span of many years, some recollections, writing of them just as I spoke of them. I could not begin without saying something of the loved ones who preceded me and who prepared my future with much intelligence and love.

To my dear cousin Pierre Lafond, who, since his childhood, has been so much a part of my life, I dedicate this little book of recollections.

Fig. 1 — Alice Dupré, Jeanne Chauvière, Albert Dupré, Marcel Dupré.

MY FAMILY

I was born in Rouen, in a house in the rue du Vert-Buisson, the third of May, 1886, into a family of musicians and organists.

My paternal grandfather, Aimable Dupré, was equally gifted for drawing and music. He had a good ear, but not much technique, having chosen music rather late in life. He had a charming tenor voice and, in addition to piano and organ, played rather well a brass instrument, the bugle, and also some clarinet. He took some courses at the School of Design and at the School of Music. It was at the latter where he met my maternal grandfather, and where their friendship began.

I treasure several of his charming sketches. His rather large blue eyes were a bit frightening, but he was an extremely gentle man. He gave me piano lessons, and when I practiced well, he would sketch something for me, anything I asked for. First he was organist at Saint-Nicaise in Rouen, then, until his death, at Saint-Maclou.

My paternal grandmother, Marie Dupré, also gifted in music, was the daughter of the Socialist Théodore Visinet, a practicing lawyer in Paris, editor-in-chief, in 1828, of a Rouen newspaper, founder of Rouen's first gas company, and chief magistrate, in 1848, of the Orne region.

My maternal grandfather, Etienne Chauvière, was my father's best friend. He had a superb bass voice, had a fine stage presence, and took up, at first, an operatic career. His principal roles were: Marcel in *The Huguenots* (the source of my first name), the leading role in *Robert the Devil (Robert le Diable)* (my mother was named Alice after a character in this opera), the third Anabaptist in *The Prophet (Le Prophète)*, the cardinal in *The Jewess (La Juive)*, etc. He did a season in Brest, two in Amsterdam, then, refusing an engagement in New Orleans, he abandoned opera and returned to Rouen. There he was appointed choir director at Saint-Patrice, a post he held for thirty years.

During my childhood and adolescence (I was eighteen years old when he died) I was his "pal." He taught me solfeggio, plainsong and music copying, spending long hours by my side to watch over my progress.

My father, Albert Dupré, after completing academic studies at the Lycée Corneille — receiving a diploma in letters, one in science, and a gold medal in mathematics — but loving music above all else, decided to devote himself to the organ. He studied for seven years with the great organist Alexandre Guilmant, going each month for a lesson in Meudon, a town where destiny would lead me later. During these years he had to find an occupation which, while providing for his needs, left him enough time for his organ study. He obtained a position at the Lycée Corneille as a prefect. (Later he became the music teacher in the same school; and the great André Maurois, who was one of his pupils, speaks of my father in his *Memoirs.*) Around this time my father was betrothed to Alice Chauvière, and after seven years, in 1848, they were married in the Church of Saint-Maclou. Guilmant was both witness and organist.

My mother was a born musician, gifted in every way. She began, as a small child, to take piano and harmony lessons with Aloÿs Klein, organist at Rouen's cathedral — a remarkable musician who had been my father's first teacher. She herself began, at the age of thirteen, to give music lessons, and she earned two francs an hour. She related to me that each pupil would give her, after the lesson, a beautiful, brand-new silver coin, which her mother guarded reverently. It was thus she accumulated a dowry of seventeen hundred francs.

At home she practiced constantly, either the piano or the cello. She started to study this latter instrument under the following circumstances.

The house in the rue du Vert-Buisson was already, from the time of my grandparents Chauvière, a center for music. It was, at the same time, in spite of their modest means, a place where several excellent musicians, some living in poverty, gathered frequently. After a simple meal, the evening was devoted to music — trios, quartets, quintets. Among the players were Gérard Hekking, father of the cellist André Hekking, and Engelmann, a German cellist living in Rouen. The latter gentleman, in his youth, was a member of the trio organized by Mendelssohn to tour Germany.

Engelmann, having seen for himself my mother's exceptional gifts — she was only nine when he heard her play the piano — offered to teach her the cello, seeking a way to repay the hospitality he received from my grandfather. He discerned immediately the musical ear of his little pupil, who was able to tune the four strings to perfection. She read at sight the most difficult music, and she was able to transpose easily. Her hands were small, but she developed quickly a perfect legato, a beautiful tone and a virtuoso's technique. All who heard her play the cello remarked how very much her playing touched their hearts.

I treasure the beautiful instrument of Niccolo Amati, Stradivarius' master, which her parents, by dint of saving, gave her on her eighteenth birthday.

She was the brightest star of many artistic events in Rouen, and she helped to instill a love of music in an entire generation.

My mother's sister, Jeanne Chauvière, gifted with a beautiful contralto voice, devoted her life, which she shared with us, to teaching voice and to giving numerous vocal recitals.

This is the milieu in which I grew up.

Fig. 2 — Rue du Vert-Buisson, a painting by Henri Vignet.

LA RUE DU VERT-BUISSON

After their marriage my parents rented a little house, 16 rue du Vert-Buisson, which belonged to my grandparents Chauvière, who were living next door at number 12.

My mother's small dowry was used to buy a Pleyel baby grand piano. On the first floor there was a sitting room. Here my father placed the piano, attaching to it a pedal-board* which had belonged to his first teacher, Aloÿs Klein. I had, from the age of two, my own little corner. Seated in my small bamboo chair (which went everywhere with me), I was captivated by my father's pedal playing, and I began to dream about playing the organ.

Four years later my father was able to buy the house at number 12. (My grandparents stayed on with us there.) Immediately he started to build a music room, my grandfather willingly sacrificing a part of his garden, which he loved very much, for the project. To inaugurate this room, my father, having organized and rehearsed a group of singers, staged the "Grail" scene from Act I of *Parsifal*. The effect of the scene's off-stage chorus was very good, thanks to a small circular window in the ceiling which concealed a trap door leading to a room on the second floor. The off-stage chorus and a harmonium were placed in this room, and this arrangement helped to create the mystical atmosphere required in the scene.

A piano with an attached pedal-board is known as a pedal-piano. It is used to practice organ music when a pipe organ is not available.

MY CHILDHOOD

One of my first recollections is from the year 1890. I was four years old. Widor, whose name I had frequently heard mentioned, was about to come to Rouen to play the opening concert on the new organ in Saint-Ouen. For this occasion he had composed his *Symphonie-Gothique.* This event was on everyone's lips, and I awaited impatiently the big day, thinking I would be permitted to attend the recital. Cruel disappointment! I was entrusted to our maid Joséphine — Fifi to us. (A wonderful human being, she had started to work for my grandmother Dupré at the age of thirteen. Fifi never left our family, and when she died at ninety-three, she had helped rear three generations of children.) During the concert Fifi was to take me for a walk in the park surrounding the church. But, being very devout, she decided to attend Benediction [which preceded the recital], and we entered the church as the first bell sounded. While she was praying, I was gone in a flash, stealing my way to a nearby staircase which led to the organ loft. (I knew the way very well, for my father had taken me into the organ loft several times while the new instrument was being installed. I was petrified the first time I saw the huge four-manual console!) When I reached the organ loft, out of breath, Widor had just begun to play. All around him there was a group of organists. I heard someone whisper, "Oh! the little Dupré." My father, fortunately, was on the other side of the console and had not seen me. I did not budge, my eyes glued on the hands of the maître. When he stopped playing, I went right up to him. "You play very well, Monsieur, but my papa plays well also." Laughter all round, except for my embarrassed father, who apologized to Widor, the latter gently agreeing with me. The whole town knew the story. Of course, I received my little scolding when we returned to the house; but secretly, I was quite pleased with my little expedition.

As for poor Fifi, when she raised her head and noticed that I had disappeared, it did not take her long to figure out which way I had gone, for she had heard me say over and over again during our walk in the park, "I want to climb to the organ loft." She clambered up the stairs after me, and when she found me, she gave me a good scolding. I threw my arms around her and was forgiven on the spot.

I learned later that the great organ builder Aristide Cavaillé-Coll had been in the loft, impatiently awaiting Widor's opinion of his instrument. To his question, Widor replied, "It is a work of art worthy of Michelangelo." (And it is indeed that!)

Next, Cavaillé-Coll asked my father, "How much do you believe the organ cost me?"

"Everyone says that you were paid ninety thousand francs."

"Correct, but between you and me, it cost one hundred eight thousand. However, I have no regrets, for I wished to build something truly wonderful."

Fig. 3 — Marcel Dupré, age four.

My childhood, so happy until now, underwent a terrible ordeal. At the age of five I contracted osteomyelitis in the right collar bone. One operation took place; then six months later, a second one, to remove the diseased part of the bone. There followed many months of suffering. For a long time the memory of the daily painful dressings was a living nightmare. Each morning my brave Fifi came downstairs from my grandmother's apartment. She always held a mysterious small package, the sight of which always gave me a moment of joy. I had had the idea of building a small altar in my room at which I could celebrate in May the Month of Mary. Thanks to Fifi's small packages, my altar grew richer each day. At first there was a small statue of the Virgin Mary, then some candles and a censer, next some small vases with flowers, and finally a cruet, a chalice, and several tiny objects on a lilliputian ladder. When the month of May arrived, the light from my candle-lit altar filled me with wonder. I have always kept these dear relics, which brought happiness much later to my grandchildren.

It took a whole year to recover my health. My wonderful godfather, Jules Lesueur, a Rouen merchant, helped me regain my strength. Almost every day he took me for a ride in his horsedrawn carriage, and I was able to breathe the pure air of the nearby forests. (He loved horses very much, and I can remember his beautiful mare Javanaise, who was the object of my admiration.)

Fig. 4 — Organ, Saint-Ouen, Rouen

THE CHAPEL OF SAINT-LOUIS

The rue du Vert-Buisson opens on to a little rectangular square planted with trees, the place de la Rouge-mare, so named because a bloody battle was fought there in 953. The combined armies of Louis d'Outremer, King of France, and Louis d'Othon, Emperor of Germany, were defeated by the army of Richard-Sans-Peur, Duke of Normandy.

On this square rises a charming eighteenth-century edifice, the Chapel of Saint-Louis, which had been part of an ancient Benedictine convent before becoming a police station in 1792. It had been abandoned for many years when my father, who had always dreamed of organizing a choral society, asked the town authorities to rent it to him. At his own expense he had the roof repaired, and he himself took charge of constructing a floor, a stage and a gallery. Most of the work was done at night, the days being filled with giving music lessons; and I remember seeing my father, my grandfather and a friend of theirs on their knees, nailing in place a parquet floor with the speed and skill of professionals.

My father presented choral and orchestral concerts in this chapel. The most memorable performance for me was the inaugural program in 1892, at which César Franck's oratorio *Ruth* was performed. (My role was brilliant! I had to go on stage in a beautiful new suit to offer a bouquet of flowers to the leading singer. I was six years old, and was a great success!)

Seven years later the city retracted the lease in order to turn the chapel into a storehouse for brooms and wheelbarrows. The loss was a terrible blow to my father.

In the years following, the chapel, totally abandoned, presented a distressing sight. But I am happy to have learned recently that the municipality of Rouen has begun to restore it.

MY FIRST PIANO LESSONS

Needless to say, throughout the year I was sick and part of the next one, any work at the piano was out of the question. I had learned to read music while a small child and had acquired, thanks to my grandfather Chauvière, some understanding of solfeggio. That was all. Now I did not delay in making up for lost time.

My godfather, wanting me to spend two months in the fresh air, surprised my family by renting a house for us at the seaside village of Saint-Valéry-en-Caux, where he owned property. He even moved a piano there so that I could begin to study this instrument. I was seven years old, and had already put my hands on the piano keyboard many times, discovering chords that I thought splendid. (In reality, I knew nothing!)

My father gave me a half-hour lesson every morning. At the first one he put on the music rack the *Alphabet* of Le Couppey, a volume of twenty-five one-page pieces, each having a letter of the alphabet as a title. I sight-read the first piece, "A," after a fashion; then I practiced it for a short while under my father's direction. At my second lesson the next day, he opened the book to the first page.

"But it is not necessary to play this piece. I already know it."
"You know it? All right, play it anyway!"

And I complied, playing it by heart without an error. My father did not flinch and seemed to take my accomplishment in stride. The second piece was begun, and so forth until the end of the book. In twenty-five days I was able to play the twenty-five pieces from memory.

(I inherited my mother's memory. I found it quite natural to memorize everything I learned. Consequently, I was taken aback several years later — I was fifteen years old — when my father's good friend, the famous bacteriologist Charles Nicolle, questioned me about the way my memory functioned.

14

"What happens when you recall a page of music? Do you hear all of it in your head?"

"Yes."

"Do you remember the fingerings?"

"Yes."

"Do you follow the music in your mind's eye?"

"Yes."

"Very good, you lucky chap. You possess all three memories: auditory, tactile, and visual.")

When I returned from Saint-Valéry, a big surprise awaited me in Rouen — a nice reward for my accomplishment at the piano. In my room I found a little one-stop harmonium which had been used previously by my grandfather Chauvière for rehearsing the children of the choir at Saint-Patrice. It had been relegated to the attic for many years, but now it had been restored. My little room was like a cathedral to me, one in which Fifi and I celebrated, the following May, the Month of Mary.

I began organ lessons at this time, and I also entered the third year at the Lycée Corneille.

ARISTIDE CAVAILLÉ-COLL

I have already mentioned the name of Cavaillé-Coll. He was a good friend of my family. The beginning of this friendship was both unexpected and amusing. My grandfather Dupré received a visit each year from a merchant from the region of Gaillac, and he always ordered a quarter-cask of white wine from him. During one of his visits the merchant noticed a little organ in the living room. (This instrument had been built by my grandfather himself. After his death it was placed in the village church in Cour-Cheverny, and it finished its "career" in the chancel of Saint-Nicolas in Blois. A bomb destroyed it there in 1940.)

"Well, well! You have an organ."
"Are you interested in organs?"
"Not I, but my cousin builds them."
"What is his name?"
"Aristide Cavaillé-Coll."

Amazing! Grandfather recognized the name of the man who had already demonstrated his inventive genius in the domain of organ building.

As a matter of fact, Aristide Cavaillé-Coll's family came from Gaillac, in the district called the Tarn. His great-granduncle, a Dominican priest, built and repaired organs in the eighteenth century. His grandfather and father were also organ builders. The latter moved to Montpellier where Aristide, his second son, was born on the fourth of February, 1811. Cavaillé-Coll was, therefore, a contemporary of Chopin, born in 1809; of Schumann, 1810; of Liszt, 1811; and of Wagner, 1813.

Cavaillé-Coll was twenty-two when Rossini, passing through Montpellier, made his acquaintance and had several conversations with him. Astonished by his intelligence, his knowledge, and his gifts, and sensing his genius, Rossini advised Aristide's father to send him to Paris. He promised to introduce him to all those who

Fig. 5 — Aristide Cavaillé-Coll.

would be able to help him. And he kept his word.

It took Cavaillé-Coll four days by coach to reach the capital. He was immediately introduced to eminent members of the Académie des Sciences. He pursued scientific studies, and later, upon the advice of the physicist Berton, he entered a contest to win the contract for the construction of a large organ in the Basilica of Saint-Denis. In three days he worked out a plan so remarkable that it won; but the members of the commission hesitated to award him the contract because of his age — he was only twenty-three! It was Thiers, a minister in the government, who, after getting information about him from Montpellier, signed the contract.

Saint-Denis was the first large organ built by Cavaillé-Coll. There he utilized his first inventions: harmonic pipes, sounding an octave higher than regular pipes, which introduced a magnificent new tone color; and the pneumatic lever (developed in collaboration with the English organ builder Charles Barker), which permits all manuals in a tracker-action organ to be coupled together without increasing the weight of the key action. These innovations amazed the members of the commission.

Saint-Denis can be considered the first of his masterpieces. Alas, for many years, because of lack of maintenance, this organ has been in a lamentable condition. But it appears there is an effort under way now to restore it.

After Saint-Denis, many contracts for new organs followed: Notre-Dame-de-Lorette, Saint-Roch, the Madeleine, Saint-Vincent-de-Paul and Sainte-Clotilde; then the cathedrals in Saint-Brieuc and Nancy.

There was also the contract for a small organ for the Paris Opéra. One day the director of the Opéra summoned Cavaillé-Coll.

"I know that our new organ cannot be ready for the première of *Faust* by young Gounod. What are we going to do?"
"I shall install a temporary organ. I have one in my workshop that is almost finished."
"But I have no money for this."

"What does that matter? It will not cost you anything."

Perplexed, yet overjoyed, not knowing quite how to thank him, the director offered Cavaillé-Coll free admission to the Opéra for the rest of his life.

"You will have two interesting companions in your box: Berlioz and Meyerbeer."

Cavaillé-Coll recounted that at the first performance of *Faust,* Meyerbeer, who was enraptured by the end of the "garden" scene, wanted Berlioz to go with him to congratulate Gounod. Recalcitrant at first, Berlioz finally accompanied him... reluctantly. (This story was told to me by Widor, who had heard it from his friend Rossini.)

Cavaillé-Coll introduced other innovations at Saint-Sulpice in 1862 and at Notre-Dame in 1867. Among these were: diverse wind pressures, partitioning of wind chests to improve the wind supply to the pipes, and a pneumatic combination action to facilitate the preparation of several different combinations of stops.

The creative genius of Cavaillé-Coll, always in evidence, did not prevent his having the greatest respect for older instruments. The memory of François Clicquot, almost a contemporary of his grandfather Jean-Pierre Cavaillé, was dear to him. When he had to rebuild an organ of Clicquot, he retained as many pipes as possible, repairing them rather than recasting them.

His last two masterpieces were Saint-Sernin in Toulouse and Saint-Ouen in Rouen (1890).

Albert Peschard, organist of the Abbaye aux Hommes (Saint-Etienne) in Caen and a physics teacher at that city's lycée, invented the electro-magnet used in organ key-chest actions. He approached Cavaillé-Coll, hoping to collaborate with him, as Barker had. But Cavaillé-Coll declined in these moving words: "I am old, I am sick, and I am poor. I am unable even to think about undertaking such an extensive project. These things are for the future." He had, therefore, foreseen the numerous refinements that were to be made in organ construction, thanks to electricity.

Cavaillé-Coll remains the inspired voicer, whose claim to fame is that he endowed France with instruments which, by the beauty of their various timbres and the majesty of their ensembles, are marvels.

The friendship which developed between my family and Cavaillé-Coll was so close that one can understand, aside from my admiration as a musician, how very much I cherish his memory. I was thirteen years old when he died on the thirteenth of October, 1899.

THE LITTLE THEATER

To entertain his children, my grandfather Dupré built a small theater where marionettes played *Sleeping Beauty (La Belle au Bois Dormant)*.

In turn, my father got the idea to build one of his own. He began to work on a miniature set during vacations — a castle for the second act of *Lohengrin*. Since we did not yet have electricity, all the lighting effects, which turned out to be ravishing, were realized with gas lamps, using shades of colored glass.

I am a bit embarrassed to say that I had the audacity to beg my father to stage *The Temptation of Saint Anthony (La Tentation de Saint-Antoine)*, the very same marionette show that was staged every year at Rouen's Saint-Romain Fair.

Our marionettes, beautifully fashioned, were delightful; I followed the construction of the set and the characters with great interest.

Our first performance of *The Temptation of Saint Anthony*, quite impressive, took place the day after my school's commencement exercises. (I had won five first prizes. I was quite proud of this success, for the preceding year my report card carried the comment: "an idle mind.") My father worked on his theater for seven years. It was really a marvelous little thing. Alas, the house was ransacked during World War II, and we have only a few vestiges of the charming little theater.

Fig. 6 — The "little theater" of Albert Dupré.

MY FIRST PUBLIC APPEARANCES

It was in June 1894, when I was eight years old, that I had my first contact with the public. The occasion was the inauguration of a small chancel organ in Elbeuf's Church of the Immaculate Conception. My father was organist there for twenty-five years prior to his appointment as organist at Rouen's Saint-Ouen. The program was in the afternoon, and I opened it, playing the main organ at the rear of the church. Cavaillé-Coll, who had built the new instrument, had arrived the evening before. During dinner at Cavaillé-Coll's hotel, my father began to be concerned about what he would do with me the next morning during the rehearsal of the featured work, a symphony for chorus and orchestra. He would be conducting the chorus, my mother would be playing the cello, and my aunt, singing.

"I think it best that Marcel remain at home," said my father.
"Entrust him to me," intervened Cavaillé-Coll, "and we shall take a walk along the Seine." Turning towards me, he said,
"Would you like that?"
"Oh! yes, Monsieur," I replied, filled with delight!

That night, while putting me to bed, my mother showered me with advice.
"You know Monsieur Cavaillé-Coll is old (he was eighty-three). Do not go running along the river, do not upset him, and finally, be careful not to dirty your shoes."
"But whom do you take me for?" I replied. "We shall talk about organs." And, in effect, this great man, walking with little steps, my hand in his, deigned to answer all my questions about the organs of Saint-Sulpice and Notre-Dame (instruments I had often heard discussed), patiently explaining to me everything he knew I could understand.

The program was scheduled to start at three o'clock in the afternoon. Cardinal Sourieu, archbishop of Rouen, would preside; and, at his arrival, I was to play Bach's Prelude and Fugue in E minor for the procession. My father and I were at the main organ by a quarter to three. Several minutes later my father went downstairs to see if everything was in place. He told me to sit still, and not to play before he returned. So I sat still. Suddenly I saw the organ blower running toward his pump. Then I heard the three raps made by the verger to announce the arrival of the cardinal. Without hesitating, I began to play. A few seconds later my father returned, quite out of breath, and he sat next to me without saying one word. When I finished, he said,

"I told you to wait for me."

"I know, but I could not let the cardinal enter the church without music."

The next day I overheard my father say to my mother: "The little one can take care of himself, can he not?"

The following year I again participated in a program with my father: the inauguration of the organ in Saint-Etienne, Elbeuf. In the rectory, before lunch was served, the cardinal, who was once again to preside at the ceremony, asked, "But where is my little organist?" Proud, beaming with joy, with a child's lack of inhibitions, I ran to him, nestling against his red robes.

I often accompanied my father to Elbeuf on Sundays. We lunched at the rectory and, after dessert, I was permitted to play in the garden. My biggest thrill was to get astride a bicycle and circle the stone walk at full speed, for, though I loved the organ above all, I also loved to have fun!

****

During the summer of 1896 there was a large exposition in Rouen. For this event an organ with thirty stops was installed in a large hall. Guilmant played the first program, and concerts were held there throughout the duration of the fair. On one of the programs my father performed a Handel concerto; and I, too, participated, playing Bach's Fugue in G minor ("Little") and a piece by Guilmant.

24

It was to be my first appearance upon a stage. My mother gave me a few lessons in deportment, teaching me to walk without rushing and to bow nicely. But I was not frightened. My only concern was what Guilmant and Widor would think of my playing. Both were present at the Fair (Widor to give a concert of his own compositions), and they would be attending the program.

Fig. 7 – Manuscript: *Prière*, Op. 0.001, by Marcel Dupré

ANTON RUBINSTEIN

Let us return to the year 1894. The famous Russian pianist Anton Rubinstein came to Rouen to attend the first performance in France of his opera *Nero*. I had often heard my parents speak of him. They had been to Paris several times to hear his recitals at the Châtelet, and they had wonderful memories of his interpretations of the *Appassionata*, Berlioz's *Roi des Aulnes* (transcribed by Liszt), Schumann's Symphonic Variations, and Chopin's Sonata in B-flat minor.

After the performance of *Nero*, my mother took a card and some flowers to the hotel where Rubinstein was staying. The moment he received them, he sent for us. Seeing the tiny tot that I was, he placed me upon his knee. He wanted to know all about me, keeping us a rather long time. I can still see his enormous hands, which impressed me very much. As we left, he said to my parents, "So you want to rear a musician?" Then he added sadly, "The poor chap."

I did not understand why he called me a "poor chap," so I asked my parents as we were leaving,

"What did he mean by that?"

"He meant that a musician's life is very difficult — that a musician must work very, very hard."

"Oh! That is all right. I like to work hard!"

Fig. 8 – Organ of Albert Dupré

THE ORGAN, RUE DU VERT-BUISSON

In July 1895 great changes took place in our house. A workshop at the back of our garden was demolished, and in its place, a charming panelled music room was built. The pedal-piano was placed there. The little theatre was taken from the attic and put in the basement, where it was better placed. We now had electricity (though very costly) for the lighting effects; and we did several performances of excerpts from Act II of *Lohengrin*.

It was at this time that a wonderful relationship developed between my grandfather Chauvière and me. (It was to continue until his death on the second of February, 1905.) He was both guide and constant companion in my practice. In winter he lit the fire each morning, and when I came home from school at ten o'clock (I was excused from certain classes), I found a nice fire in the fireplace, and my grandfather waiting to help me.

Some time afterwards, an old stump was removed from the back of the garden, and a larger music room was built. In spite of the loss of the Chapel of Saint-Louis, my father had not given up his dream of having a choral society, but first of all, he wanted to have an organ. The first meeting with Cavaillé-Coll took place when the room was almost finished. (He came to Rouen with his foreman.) I overheard, quivering with delight, what was said about the construction of the instrument; and during lunch, with a child's audacity, I uttered suddenly,

"Monsieur Cavaillé-Coll, will there be towers on the organ case?"

"You want towers? You shall have them! I shall have two designed for you, each with three large pipes, and I shall send you the blueprint in a few days." My mother's startled eyes had no effect on me. I was so happy. I would lie in wait for the mailman each morning. Finally a packet addressed to me arrived: a lovely water-colored design of the proposed organ case — with my towers. Beaming, I wrote a thank-you note to Cavaillé-Coll. (I have always kept this sketch in the little pavilion in our garden, our "museum," where numerous photographs of organs that I played in the course of my career are displayed.)

While the organ was being constructed at Cavaillé-Coll's Paris factory on the avenue du Maine, my father finished the room where the instrument was to be placed. At last, on the fifteenth of September, 1896, the organ arrived, crated in various sections, and it took a month to assemble it. What wonderful days! Every morning at seven o'clock, when I heard the workmen arrive, I leaped from my bed, dressed quickly, and started downstairs. Occasionally my mother stopped me in the hallway, making me return to my room to finish washing my face!

Four steps at a time I leaped down the stairs to join the workmen and, under their watchful eyes, I did little things for them, such as passing tools from one to another and helping to assemble parts for the keyboards. Above all, I stared at the great voicer Garnier while he regulated the pipes, working with one pipe until he obtained the exact timbre and pitch. I was astonished at his great patience. In this manner, though still a child, I was introduced to organ building, and I fell in love with it, so much so that several years later I confided to my father one day that I could not decide whether to become an organist or an organ builder. I was brought to my senses by one of his comments, "My poor fellow, you can do absolutely nothing in mathematics. How would you be able to do the necessary calculations in order to make a blueprint of an organ?" His argument settled my dilemma.

When the organ was completed, I declared joyfully to my father,
"Now I can practice the organ and put the piano aside somewhat!"
"Nothing of the sort," he answered. "From now on, for every three quarters of an hour at the piano, you will have the right to a quarter of an hour at the organ." I hung my head. This was my practice schedule for quite some time, and I understood much later that he had been right.

Fig. 9 – Marcel Dupré, about 1900.

Our instrument, which had two manuals and eleven stops, is now the small chancel organ in the Rouen Cathedral. When I suggested to the priest in charge, Monsignor Jean Delamare, that he might remove the two gold letters – A.D. (for Albert Dupré) – which Cavaillé-Coll had put on the pediment of the organ case, he answered, "Not at all. We shall translate A.D. as *Ave Domine.*" It is a poignant moment for me each time I see these dear initials.

PAUL PARAY

We spent our vacations at Le Tréport in 1895 and 1896. In the church, which dominates the town, there was a fine small Cavaillé-Coll organ. The organist was Auguste Paray, father of the great conductor Paul Paray. Paul was my junior by three weeks.

As soon as we arrived in Le Tréport, Monsieur Paray came to find my father, offering to put the organ at his disposal so that he could continue my lessons. "I give Paul a lesson every morning at ten o'clock. The organ will be free for you at eleven." Thus mornings were devoted to lessons, but Paul and I played together in the afternoons.

Monsieur Paray also directed a brass ensemble in which Paul, because of his wonderfully supple wrists, played snare drum. Paul paraded at the head of the formation, his eyes glued on his father's baton. He aroused my admiration.

It was at Le Tréport that I met Dallier, titular organist of Saint-Eustache in Paris before he succeeded Gabriel Fauré at La Madeleine. One Sunday he came to play at the church in Le Tréport, and I went with my father to the organ loft. I was dazzled by Dallier's playing, but after his postlude, when I saw him close the lid of the console, my eyes filled with tears.

"What is wrong, my fine fellow?" Dallier asked.
"Papa does not want me to play this morning," I replied.
"Do you want to play? Come here."
And without looking at my father, I sat down quickly on the bench.

ALEXANDRE GUILMANT

Guilmant's name has already appeared several times in these pages, but now I wish to bring together my recollections of this great maître, to whom I owe so much. When he saw me for the first time I was three days old. Returning from a trip to Les Andelys, where he had inaugurated an organ, he stopped in Rouen to visit my mother. (My birth had been somewhat difficult, and at the sight of the little "misshapen" face that had just seen the light of day, my father exclaimed, "I just knew I would have a little monster." One must believe that three days later the "monster" had changed to something quite different.) As Guilmant bent over my cradle, he showed signs of joy. And after taking my little hand in his and examining my fingers, he said, "We shall have an organist here." My mother, who years later described the scene to me, was delighted with Guilmant's prediction.

When did I see Guilmant for the first time? It would be difficult to say. But I heard much about him from my father, who had been his pupil for seven years. I knew that Guilmant was interested in me and in my studies. He honored me by coming to Rouen to be present for my first Communion in the chapel of the Lycée Corneille, he himself playing the harmonium for the service.

Speaking of my first Communion, I am unable to refrain from relating a little story. My parents asked what I would like to have in honor of this occasion.

"A trip to Paris," I replied, "to visit the Botanical Gardens; to climb the Eiffel Tower; to hear the organs at La Trinité (where Guilmant was organist), Saint-Sulpice and Notre-Dame; to see a performance of *Die Meistersinger* at the Opéra (the schedule of performances had already been announced); and to go to lunch at Guilmant's home."

"Is that all?" my father said, laughing. "All right, except for the last item on your agenda. One does not invite oneself to lunch.

Fig. 10 — Alexandre Guilmant.

But we shall ask Guilmant if it is possible to visit him in Meudon."

We did not wait long for an answer. "Come for lunch," he wrote. I was in heaven. But on that day I came down quickly from my "paradise" when, after lunch, Guilmant said to me, "You have begun to study fugue. I am going to give you a very simple subject upon which you are going to improvise." Trembling, I sat down at the organ; and while playing, I thought to myself that I was paying dearly for my lunch. When I had finished, Guilmant said, "Good! For one of your age it is not bad. Later on I shall accept you in my class at the Conservatoire." I felt better.

We visited the other places on my list. In the organ loft at Saint-Sulpice, Widor placed me next to him on the bench and explained to me many details of the plan of the organ. I never thought for one moment that he would call me one day to be his assistant [and later his successor], and that this wonderful instrument would become for me, as it was for him, one of the greatest joys of my life.

But I must return to Guilmant. Thanks to him, I took an important step. One day my father told me that the Church of Saint-Vivien in Rouen was about to get a new organ.

"Who will be the organist?"
"Probably the young lady who plays the harmonium."
"How is that? Did you not submit my name as a candidate?"
"No, I will not let you take an organ position before you have studied with Guilmant."
"What is the salary?"
"Four hundred francs a year."
"So, with this amount I could go to Meudon for my lessons, just as you did."
"I was nineteen years old when I travelled to Meudon to study with Guilmant. Do you believe that I would let you, at eleven, go there alone?"

I kept quiet, but I did not consider myself beaten. I went to find my mother and, becoming the best possible little wheedler, I pleaded with her to speak to my father. She did and the result was that he wrote Guilmant to ask his opinion. I had won round one.

Each morning I waited impatiently for the mail to arrive; but I had not long to wait: "Marcel is right," wrote Guilmant. "Nothing would be better for him than to be the regular organist of Saint-Vivien. From now on he will be my pupil. You can bring him to Meudon once a month." And so, as he had been to my father for seven years, Guilmant was, for ten years, both my friend and teacher, never charging for a lesson.

He was a wonderful maître, being extremely severe in seeking perfection, but having such patience and gentleness that, child that I was, I never minded being stopped (sometimes at each measure) for the slightest detail. A wrong note was followed by a "put on your glasses, Marcel," which made me pay closer attention. The lesson lasted two hours — piano, organ, harmony, counterpoint, and improvisation — but it seemed very short.

I was appointed organist of Saint-Vivien the twentieth of October, 1897, before the organ was finished.

The first recital on the new organ was played the following year on the twenty-eighth of June by Guilmant. He insisted that I play the first piece on the program, Bach's Prelude and Fugue in E minor.

Guilmant was a great, a very great organist, who brought honors to France. He was invited to play forty recitals in the United States at the Saint Louis Exposition, for which a huge organ had been built. He was a great success. Later, he repeated his success in the course of an American tour. The school in New York which carries his name, Guilmant Organ School, keeps his memory alive. [When Dupré wrote this, the Guilmant Organ School was still in existence.]

His marvelous Anthology of Old Masters of the Organ, published in several volumes, as well as his numerous original compositions, are a precious heritage for organists.

Fig. 11 — Organ, Saint-Vivien, Rouen

THE VILLA JULIA-MARIE

When my godfather learned of my appointment to Saint-Vivien, he was very proud and wanted to reward me. He bought a house at Saint-Valéry-en-Caux, and, having put it in good condition, made it available. We spent all our vacations there from 1898 until the war in 1940.

Fig. 12 — Villa Julia-Marie.

Half way down a hillside garden, where our daughter Marguerite took her first steps, there stood an old barn which we converted into a music room. A practice pedal-board was kept there, and each summer a piano was brought from Rouen. There I worked and composed each summer. It was there, in 1912, that Louis Vierne, who spent several vacations with us, wrote his Third Organ Symphony, which he kindly dedicated to me.

Each afternoon we played music for numerous friends who were spending their vacations at Saint-Valéry.

During one summer vacation I met Amable Massis, now one of my oldest friends. (Later he became Inspector-General for music.) He was seven years old and was very gifted in playing the violin.

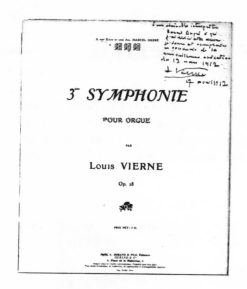

To my great interpreter Marcel Dupré, to whom I have dedicated this work, I give this copy in appreciation of his marvelous performance on March 12, 1912.
L. Vierne
April 17, 1912

Fig. 13 — Title Page, Third Organ Symphony by Louis Vierne.

Many composers and performers came to the villa. One of the most regular visitors was my friend Emmanuel Bondeville, also from Rouen. He came each summer to show me his most recent compositions. It was there that we sight read his symphonic poems for the first time — *Le Bal des Pendus, Ophélie,* and *Marine,* all of which were inspired by poems of Rimbaud. Their successful performance by the Lamoureux Orchestra under the direction of Albert Wolff marked the debut of an outstanding career.

It was in 1915 that my father introduced the young Emmanuel Bondeville to Widor, who had come to Rouen to conduct his *Salvum fac,* for organ and trumpets, in Saint-Ouen. My father hardly suspected that he was presenting to the incumbent Secrétaire Perpétuel of the Académie des Beaux-Arts,* the man who would assume the same position some fifty years later.

The Académie des Beaux-Arts is one of five divisions in the Institut de France. The others are: the Académie des Inscriptions et Belles-Lettres, the Académie des Sciences, the Académie des Sciences morales et politiques, and the celebrated Académie française. Each académicien *is elected by his peers for life.*

L'ACCORD PARFAIT

Immediately after the organ had been installed at number 12 rue du Vert-Buisson, my father decided to organize a choral society. He had frequently formed choruses in the past, but they had functioned only intermittently. It was necessary to find a name for this new organization. Each member placed his choice in a large urn.

The name, L'Accord Parfait (The Perfect Accord), pleased everyone. The group functioned for thirty years. Rehearsals were held every Friday evening, my mother at the piano and I, occasionally, at the organ.

The first work performed in public was Gounod's *Gallia*; followed by, in the course of many years, Handel's *Messiah*; Mendelssohn's *Elijah* and *Saint Paul*; Bach's *Christmas Oratorio, The Passion of our Lord According to St. John and St. Matthew*, and some of his cantatas; Haydn's *Seasons*; Dubois' *Seven Last Words*; Beethoven's *Christ on the Mount of Olives*; Brahm's *Requiem*; Fauré's *Requiem*; Paray's *Jeanne d'Arc*; Vierne's *Praxinoé* (performed at the Salle Gaveau in Paris), Berlioz's *Childhood of Christ (L'Enfance du Christ)*, Debussy's *Blessed Demoiselle (La Demoiselle Elue)*, and I shall stop here. What a lesson for me!

My father had also organized an amateur orchestra. It rehearsed every Monday evening.

As the chorus and orchestra grew larger — to over one hundred members — our music room became too small. The remaining third of the garden was sacrificed in order to build a larger music room. (The organ was relocated, of course, in the new room.) Two concerts were given to inaugurate the room. For the first one, the third of May, 1901, which fell on my fifteenth birthday, L'Accord Parfait sang a cantata I had composed, *Jacob's Dream (Le Songe de Jacob)*. It had not been orchestrated, so it was accompanied by by mother at the piano and by me at the organ.

The idea for this little work went back to my first Communion. One of my presents was a magnificent Bible illustrated by Gustave Doré, and I was fascinated, even obsessed, by the story of Jacob's vision. I spent many moments thinking about the marvelous ladder, whose top reached to the heavens and whose length was filled with angels ascending and descending.

I even dreamed about it in musical terms, and I revealed this fact to my parents one day. We all agreed to write a text, family style.

ACCORD PARFAIT

17e CONCERT

VENDREDI 3 MAI 1901

PREMIÈRE PARTIE

1. **Paulus** (Chœur)..................... MENDELSSOHN
   Dieu, toi qui fis les Cieux.
2. **Grande Fugue** en *sol min*................. J.-S. BACH
   M. MARCEL DUPRÉ.
3. **Quintette de Carmen**.................... BIZET
   MMmes FONTAINE et JEAN MAILLART
   Mlle J. CHAUVIÈRE.
   MM. LANQUETUIT et VANNIER.
4. **Prélude du Déluge**.............. SAINT-SAENS
   M. LAMOURY.

LA VISION DE JACOB

Scène Biblique pour Chœurs, Soli et Orchestre
Par M. MARCEL DUPRÉ
L'Archange. Mlle J. CHAUVIÈRE.
Dieu........ M. RIGAL.
Récitants. — Ténor : M. LANQUETUIT.
Baryton : M. VANNIER.
Basse : M. SAUDEGRAIN.

DEUXIÈME PARTIE

1. **Paulus**..................... MENDELSSOHN
   Chœurs : *a* Punissez l'Insolent.
   b Honneur à toi !
2. **Freyschütz** (Air d'Agathe)............. WEBER
   Mlle MARGUERITE LETOURNEUR.
3. **Motet** (Chœur)..................... RENÉ DOIRE
   Sous la direction de l'AUTEUR.

   O vos omnes qui transitis per viam, / O vous tous qui passez sur la route,
   attendite et videte si est dolor similis / considérez et voyez s'il est une dou-
   sicut dolor meus. / leur semblable à la mienne.
   Attendite universi populi et videte / Peuples de la terre, considérez mon
   dolorem meum. / affliction et voyez.

4. **Kermesse de Faust** pour Piano........... GOUNOD, St-SAENS
   M. MARCEL DUPRE.
5. **Messie**..................... HÆNDEL
   Chœurs : *a* O Divin Sauveur.
   b Alleluia.

Fig. 14 — Program: L'Accord Parfait.

The performance was a thrilling event for me. Madame Samson, the granddaughter of Boieldieu, composer of the comic opera *La Dame Blanche,* came to the first program. She became interested in me and gave my father a sum of money with which to buy a grand piano. The Erard Company showed us a magnificent concert grand piano which had been used by Paderewski for one of his concert tours, and we bought it. When the instrument arrived at our house, Madame Samson was invited to come to hear it. With what feeling and gratitude I played for her. This piano is still mine and is located in my *salle d'orgue**, and, like me, it has grown old; but it is very dear to me, and I still practice on it every morning, having such wonderful memories.

*The salle d'orgue, *or organ hall, in the Dupré home was built to house his thirty-four rank Cavaillé-Coll organ. The room seats over one hundred people.*

THE CONSERVATOIRE

Guilmant insisted that I join the piano class at the Conservatoire before becoming a member of his organ class, so he introduced me to the great piano virtuoso and teacher Louis Diémer, who entrusted me to his assistant, Lazare Lévy.

When it was time to prepare for the final examination, I went into seclusion in Saint-Germain-en-Laye, at the home of my great-uncle Georges Visinet. There I could work in peace and quiet. Eight or nine hours a day I practiced, until I could play all the difficult passages in the two required pieces: Chopin's Second Ballade and Saint-Saëns' Toccata. One day a delegation of neighbors arrived at the door to make a complaint. "We are weary of this music which never stops. It is a waste of time to persist at something in which one is not more talented." I accepted their so-called advice and made sure to keep my window shut during this unusually hot month of June 1905.

In July I obtained my first prize. Guilmant advised me to audit his course for a year before becoming a member of the class. In this way I could finish my counterpoint studies. He entrusted me to his assistant, Louis Vierne, but the latter had an accident and was obliged to cancel his teaching. Guilmant then placed me in the hands of another of his pupils, Paul Fauchet, a second prize winner in organ and a remarkable contrapuntist. I shall speak of him further along.

In January 1906 I had an accident which nearly destroyed my career as a virtuoso. In stumbling, I thrust my right hand through a glass door. My wrist slashed and losing much blood, I ran as fast as I could to the closest pharmacist, who immediately sent me to a doctor. The doctor pointed out a nerve to me. "Do you see this little 'thread'? It is the cubital nerve. It is intact. If it had been severed, you would have had three limp fingers, permanently paralyzed. You were very lucky." I was not able to use my right hand for three weeks. But I lost no time. I did my counterpoint

Fig. 15 — Marcel Dupré, about 1903.

exercises with my left hand (this change did not bother me, for I had learned to be ambidextrous at the time of my operation) and I practiced my pedal technique like a madman. At the end of twenty-one days I received permission to play again.

To get started, I decided to try to play from memory a volume of Bach's organ music. Since Guilmant had already required me to learn seven of the ten Preludes and Fugues, I had, obviously, only three left to learn. When I was ready, I played the entire book for my family in the course of an evening. It was in this way that I conceived the idea of playing, at a later date, all of Bach's organ works from memory.

The following year, 1907, I was admitted to the organ class, having studied counterpoint for a year with Paul Fauchet. I continued to see him, for we were now classmates. (Paul was at the head of our class, already having his second prize in organ.) In fact, we had to compete against each other. He continued, no less, to help me (without ever accepting the slightest remuneration), and he did it so modestly, so sincerely, that he won my admiration.

In January he said to me, "You will be qualified to play in the final competition." In February, "You are going to be second runner-up." In March, "You will be first runner-up." In April, "You will have a second prize, as I had last year." And in May, "You will have the first prize, not I." Happily, he was wrong.

The day of the competition I was the first to play (I thought this to be an unfavorable sign). As I left the hall, feeling somewhat depressed after my ordeal, someone from the panel of judges came up to me.

"Do you want to earn ten francs by playing the recessional at a wedding in a nearby church, Saint-Eugène?" he asked. "The organist is not able to stay until the end."

I accepted, for this change would help to get my mind off the competition. When I returned to the Conservatoire, I was one golden coin richer.

The results of the competition were announced a little later, and to my great joy, both Paul Fauchet and I had a first prize. The Guilmant Prize was awarded to me, and I had much difficulty convincing my dear friend to split it — a small enough token of my gratefulness. A brotherly friendship linked us until his death. At first a choir director at Saint-Pierre de Chaillot, and then a harmony teacher at the Conservatoire, his life was one of selfless service.

In October 1907 I entered Widor's class in fugue and composition. Darius Milhaud and Arthur Honegger were my classmates. In 1909 I obtained my first prize in fugue.

Fig. 16 — Nave and organ, Saint-Sulpice, Paris.

SAINT-SULPICE

While I was still a member of the organ class, Widor's assistant at Saint-Sulpice died. I was summoned by Widor himself, who, to my great suprise, asked me to be his assistant.

"But maître, I do not yet have my first prize in organ."
"I know that, but you will have it soon!"

Since he had to leave on a trip, he entrusted me with his instrument for two Sundays. He also asked me to play for a wedding the very next day at eleven o'clock.

"Be at the church a half-hour ahead of time so that I can give you the necessary instructions."
"What should I play?"
"Improvise."

The next day he showed me the various characteristics of the organ. "I leave you now. You are going to have some fun!"

After he left, I looked down into the nave to be sure he had gone. Then I took my place at the organ, filled with an indescribable feeling. Just think of it, I was going to play this organ of a hundred stops, one that I had heard and seen for the first time eight years earlier. That evening I saw Vierne, who said to me,

"This morning your prelude was in the key of B-flat, your recessional in E minor, and your postlude in B."
"How did you know that? You were there?"
"No, but 'he' reentered the church, heard everything; and said to me later, 'I shall take him,' and he even added, 'Are you sure he improvised? It seemed written.' "

CHARLES-MARIE WIDOR

I have already told the story of my first contact with Widor, who was destined to fill such a large place in my life. He had been appointed organist at Saint-Sulpice in 1869, at the age of twenty-five, upon the recommendation of Cavaillé-Coll. This appointment had some repercussions among organists. A letter of protest carrying several signatures was sent to the pastor of the parish. He immediately summoned Cavaillé-Coll. Looking over the signatures, the latter remarked that not one single name was that of an important organist. "I noticed that myself," said the pastor, and he sent for Widor. "I am appointing you temporary organist for one year, beginning on the first of January."

The following New Year's Day, Widor went to visit the pastor to present in person his best wishes for the New Year. He was hoping to have some word on his temporary status, but the subject was not even mentioned! Widor did not dare to bring it up, and the pastor appeared to have forgotten the terms of the nomination. "It is like this," Widor said to me at the end of his life, "I have been the 'temporary organist' of Saint-Sulpice for sixty-four years!"

For seven years, twice a week — Mondays and Thursdays after class — Widor took me to lunch at Foyot's (no longer there), opposite the Palais du Luxembourg. He ate in this restaurant regularly and received his friends there. A small horse-drawn carriage was always waiting for him at the door of the Conservatoire, and those rides across Paris in beautiful weather remain a delightful memory for me. Widor knew everyone at Foyot's: senators, writers, painters, the entire Parisian artistic elite. He introduced me to many of them. The painter Forain, often seated at the next table, greatly entertained me with his witty comments.

One day, when Widor and I were already at the table, I on his right, I saw Massenet coming toward us. "It is true," Widor said. "I

Fig. 17 — Charles-Marie Widor

forgot to tell you that he was joining us for lunch." I popped up like a jack-in-the-box in order to give him my place. "No, no, my boy, stay there. After all, you will not be so badly off between Widor and me." Blushing from embarrassment, I kept my place. Natural, kind, inspiring, and a delightful raconteur, Massenet captivated me with his charm. (In my youth I had often heard Massenet praised by my uncle Joseph Lafond, manager of Rouen's daily newspaper. Uncle Joseph was a friend of the composer, both having been born in the Loire Valley.)

One of my classmates, Félix Fourdrain, whose *Légende du point d'Argentan* and *Tales of Perrault (Contes de Perrault)* were performed later at the Opéra-Comique, related this moving story to me. Massenet, having learned that Félix was destitute, summoned him one day. "You will come to study with me." (An interesting detail is the fact that the composer of *Manon* lived opposite the rectory of Saint-Sulpice.) "I shall see you three times a week, at a quarter to twelve, for fifteen minutes. But you will see. I shall teach you more about composition in these fifteen minutes than others do in two hours." And when the lesson was finished, he would guide his pupil not towards the door, but towards the dining room, where a solid meal was served him. Fourdrain had tears in his eyes when relating this episode in his life.

Let us return to Widor. Talking with him was thrilling. He had met most of the great men from the declining days of Romanticism, either at the home of Madame Érard, or at the home of Madame Bertin, the wife of the French publisher who brought *Le Journal des Débats* to great prominence in the early ninteenth century.

The trips I took with Widor were a delight. Especially notable were those to Barcelona, Wiesbaden and Marseilles, where I played the organ part in his *Sinfonia Sacra*.

Like me, Widor loved to relate past experiences, and he told some wonderful stories that I have always remembered.

One dealt with Wagner. In 1876 Widor went to Bayreuth to

hear the Ring Cycle. During an intermission at a performance of *Götterdämmerung*, he suddenly found himself in the presence of Liszt, who knew of Widor's Hungarian ancestry.

"How is it, Widor, that you are at Bayreuth and you have not come to meet a fellow-countryman? And have you ever met Wagner?"

"No, maître."

"Then come with me."

At an open doorway an unexpected sight greeted their eyes. At the other end of the room, Wagner, his back toward them, fists in the air, stood shouting before a giant of a man whose size was heightened even more by a plumed helmet. The man, shouldering a spear, seemed quite unmoved by Wagner's thunderous roars. Wagner was scolding him, without a doubt for some blunder he had made in the role of Hagen. Liszt withdrew quietly. "As you can see, Widor, this is not the moment."

One of the best stories dealt with Liszt. Shortly after Cavaillé-Coll built the Trocadéro* organ for the Paris Exposition of 1878, Liszt, whom he knew and admired, and Helmholtz, the great physicist and acoustical expert, were invited to come to Paris to sit on a jury judging solo performers in the instrumental class at the Conservatoire. One morning, Widor related to me, Cavaillé-Coll burst into his apartment. "Come quickly," he said, "Liszt intends to try the Trocadéro organ. When he is finished, you can play for him. This way he can hear the instrument away from the console. Afterward we shall have lunch together." I can well imagine how excited Widor became at the thought of finding himself in the presence of this great musician. "He gave me such a warm welcome," Widor said, "that I immediately felt at ease. Liszt played the organ, admiring the magnificent timbres. Then he asked me to play one of my own compositions; he listened from the back of the auditorium." When Widor had finished playing, all three of them went to Foyot's. During lunch Liszt said to Widor:

The name "Trocadéro" is that of a fortress in Cadiz, taken by the French in 1823. They had been sent by the Holy Alliance to reestablish an absolute monarchy in Spain. The Parisian site was named in 1827 and the square was planned in 1858. The 1878 Exhibition building was replaced in 1937 by the Palais de Chaillot.

"You have been very kind to devote your morning to me, and even kinder to play for me. How can I thank you?"

"Maître, if I could hear you play the piano, even for five minutes, I would. . ."

"Five minutes, that is a very short time," replied Liszt laughing. "This is what I propose. Come to Madame Érard's country estate La Muette. I am her guest for one more week, and I practice the piano every morning from nine to twelve. When I say I "practice," I should say I play; I play to my heart's content the pieces that I love." And for six consecutive mornings Widor heard from Liszt's fingers an important portion of the piano literature, from Bach to Liszt, touching upon Mozart, Beethoven, Schubert, Schumann, Chopin, and even certain new pieces, such as *Islamey* of Balakireff. "He knew everything ever written for the piano," Widor said to me. "He never gave the impression of speed, and the music came directly from his heart. His immense hands spread over the keys like two fans and his orchestral coloring was incomparable. It is the most extraordinary recollection of my artistic career."

****

Beneath a cold appearance Widor had a warm and generous heart. I witnessed many of his acts of kindness to unfortunate artists. And he always forgot past disagreements. One day, arriving at his office in the Institut (he was Secrétaire Perpétuel of the Académie des Beaux-Arts), I found him in a jovial mood. "Come here. Listen to this letter that I just wrote. 'Sir, I can not thank you for the review you wrote of my last piece, but I have the pleasure of informing you that I have just given my approval for the aid you requested.' " The recipient of that letter never replied, but the essential point was that Widor had helped him.

The year 1933 marked the end of Widor's professional activity. His health began to fail. When my wife and I went to say goodbye before our departure for the United States, he said to us, "Come back quickly, I feel tired." Upon our return we found him very ill. He continued, however, to climb to the organ loft every Sunday, but he asked me to play the greater part of the Mass. At that time, the organ was still used during the entire length of the Offertory, and most frequently he wanted to hear a piece by Bach.

Fig. 18 — Charles-Marie Widor and Marcel Dupré.

Then, after the Mass on the last Sunday of that year, he took me to the Institut.

"Sit down. I am going to write my letter of resignation to the pastor of Saint-Sulpice."

I felt a sudden pang in my chest. "But maître, why? I am here to help you."

"I have made up my mind," he said quickly. "I have lost my strength, and, consequently, I am losing my technique."

He confided this to me so calmly that I was quite shaken. And he continued, "I have reasons to see you succeed me while I am still alive — you who have always been my disciple." We went to leave the letter at the rectory of Saint-Sulpice.

During the visit he made to his pastor shortly afterward, he said, "If I had been richer, I would have given to the parish the two pedal stops I have always wanted."

"Well, we are going to make a counter-proposal," answered the pastor. "In honor of your sixty-four years of devoted service to our parish, we are going to present these stops in your name." The firm of Cavaillé-Coll set about making them, and Widor had the joy of hearing these additions, which enlarged the instrument from 100 to 102 stops.

For yet another year he came to Saint-Sulpice to hear the organ; but being unable to climb the sixty-seven steps to the organ loft, he stayed in the nave, sitting near the pulpit, his favorite spot for listening to the organ. His health continued to deteriorate. He suffered for two years from a sort of blood infection. I went to see him often at his town house in the rue de Belloy (he vacated his bachelor quarters at the Institut at the time of his marriage). I usually found him confined to his bed, but working. A stroke having left him paralyzed on the right side, he was forcing himself to write with his left hand. About two weeks before his death, he asked me to play on the piano, instrument by instrument, two pages of the orchestra score of his *Symphonie Antique,* for he wanted to verify certain changes he was planning to make. As I left, he said, "Try to come to see me every day. Within a month it will all be over, I sense it. I have had enough of this suffering day and night. Yet, I should not complain, for I have had a wonderful life." He died in the evening on the twelfth of March, 1937, at the age of ninety-three.

That same evening, at La Trinité, we were commemorating the hundredth anniversary of Guilmant's birth. I and several other of his former pupils were presenting a concert of sacred music in which we played some works by our late maître. Widor had been very interested in the planning of this program. He passed away while the concert was taking place. Thus, these two great masters of the organ, these two leading disciples of Johann Sebastian Bach in France, are placed, day for day, within a century: 1837-1937.

Widor's last sign of affection and confidence was to designate me, along with Isidore Philipp, as his executor.

Fig. 19 — Organ case, Saint-Sulpice, Paris.

ALBERT SCHWEITZER

The name of Albert Schweitzer is closely associated with that of Widor, who, having been his organ teacher, became his friend. I met Schweitzer one evening at the home of the Comtesse de Behague, where Widor's *Sinfonia Sacra* was being played. (It was Schweitzer, who, at the time Widor was made an honorary member of the Berlin Academy, suggested that he compose a work for organ and orchestra, dedicating it to this learned society in appreciation. Widor liked the idea, and he composed the *Sinfonia Sacra*, choosing as the theme a chorale melody used by Bach, "Come, Saviour of the Gentiles.")

From time to time Schweitzer came to lunch at Foyot's with Widor, and I was there the day when he told our maître of his decision to leave for Gabon. There he planned to build a hospital to care for the African natives. Widor tried to persuade him to abandon this project, pointing out that it would mean interrupting the important work he had already undertaken, especially his research on the life and works of Bach. Schweitzer respectfully replied, "I know, maître, but God calls me to this task!" The next day at lunch I asked Widor if he had been able to convince Schweitzer to change his plans. He turned to me and said, "Well, Dupré, what can you do when a man says to you 'God calls me'?"

Schweitzer left for Gabon and we corresponded. He returned to Paris almost every two years, and he never failed to come to Saint-Sulpice. Seated beside me on the organ bench, just as he had sat with Widor, he listened to me play his favorite instrument.

He also visited us at Meudon. He told of his life at Lambaréné, of his work, and of his experiences. All of this would fill many a book. I loved the story of his attempt to raise, side by side, a baby and a monkey which had been born at the same hour on the same day. Until the age of two, the monkey learned faster than the child. Then he reached his limit, and the child began to surpass him.

Fig. 20 — Marcel Dupré and Albert Schweitzer at the organ console, Saint-Sulpice, Paris.

When they were making the film *Doctor Schweitzer*, Schweitzer asked me to play the organ in his place, using my instrument in Meudon. The great actor Pierre Fresnay portrayed the role of Schweitzer. I played, among other things, part of the Toccata from Widor's Fifth Organ Symphony; and I was amazed to see, when the recording of sound was finished, how Fresnay mimed my performance for the cameras. He had assimilated everything — gestures, and movements of the hands and the feet. I was astounded by his exact reproduction of my staccato.

Schweitzer's last visit to Saint-Sulpice is a wonderful memory for me. It was on the Feast of All Saints. After the service he asked me to go with him to the crypt in order that he might pray at Widor's tomb. We decided to go at two o'clock that afternoon. Father Lesourd went with us and recited the Lord's Prayer. Afterward, we returned to the nave of the church; and when we were alone, Schweitzer led me to the center, stopped, then, turning toward the organ loft, said to me,

"We are among the last representatives of an era when two great organists, Guilmant and Widor, pioneered a glorious future for the organ."

Then suddenly he said, "I am going to ask you something. Would you use the familiar form of address with me — the *tu?*"

Flabbergasted, I replied, "To hear you use it would delight me, but as for me, I could not. I would feel awkward."

"Yes, you could."

I made every attempt to do his bidding until the end of our conversation. We separated on the place Saint-Sulpice, and I never saw him again.

Fig. 21 — Letter from Schweitzer to Dupré.

Marcel Dupré
40 Boulevard Anatole France
Meudon, S. and O.

Lambaréné, 15 March 1962
Gabon, West Equatorial Africa

My dear friend,

Thank you for your letter of February 26, which informed me of the program on May 3. I had thought that on the occasion of the one-hundredth anniversary of the organ's dedication you would honor Widor and his predecessors at Saint-Sulpice. But I think you are right to render homage to the grand generation of French organ composers.

You ask me to write several lines for the program. Do you not think that this would appear presumptuous? I am somewhat hesitant. I shall send you the lines. You can decide whether to use them.

Your devoted friend,
Albert Schweitzer

M. Marcel Dupré
40 Bd Anatole France
Meudon S. et O

Sambarini 15.3.62
Gabon. Afrique Equatoriale
ni de Occidentale.

Cher ami. Merci de ta lettre du 26 février,
par laquelle j'apprends le programme du 3 Mai.

J'avais pensé, moi, qu'à l'occasion de ce sentenaire témoignage
hommage à Widor et ses prédécesseurs à St Sulpice. Mais
je trouve très bien ton idée de rendre hommage à la
grande génération des organistes d'orgue française.

Tu me demandes d'écrire quelques lignes pour le programme.
Mais ... Tu dis que cela pourrait paraître présomptueux? Je
suis intimidé. Difficile. Tu t'amuses à lignes. Je réfléchis ...

Bien amicalement
Albert Schweitzer

LE GRAND PRIX DE ROME

The mention of my admittance to Widor's class in fugue and composition was enough to precipitate a lengthy discussion of him and of our relationship. Now I shall return to the point in my life when I competed for the Grand Prix de Rome. (I had spent seven years in Widor's class preparing for this competition.) The competition took place at the Institut de France on the third of July, 1914, before the members of the music division of the Académie.* The eight men who were present were unable to name a winner: four of them cast their ballots for my friend Marc Delmas and four cast their ballots for me. Saint-Saëns, the ninth member and the only one who could break the deadlock, had refused to participate in Académie functions after Gustave Charpentier was elected a member. Saint-Saëns admired his ability as a musician, but he was furious with him for having used a thoroughly trite dialogue in his opera *Louise:*

". . .Hello! Is the soup ready?"
"In a moment."

Widor acted quickly. Immediately he had a message sent to Saint-Saëns, imploring him to come and break the impasse. Saint-Saëns yielded. He came and, as I learned later, voted for me. The next day the Académie met to announce the winner. (I was not acquainted, of course, with all the dealings of the evening before.) As I waited my turn in the courtyard of the Institut, the hot sun and my starched collar adding to my anxiety, I saw Saint-Saëns arrive. Behind him came the pianist Risler, whom I knew. The presence of these two great virtuosos made me nervous, for I might have to accompany my cantata *Psyche* on the piano. I ran up to Risler:

In this competition each candidate was given a cantata text to set for voice/s and orchestra. They worked behind closed doors (at the Château de Compiègne), presenting their compositions in a reading performance before members of the Académie.

"Oh, maître, not only Saint-Saëns, but you too!"

"Look here, Dupré, it is of no use to worry. Who knows how Saint-Saëns voted?"

Fig. 22 — Marcel Dupré's room in the Château de Compiègne.

After I was proclaimed the winner, the unfortunate Marc Delmas, who was competing for the ninth time, came up to me and said, "Marcel, I am very disappointed, but I like you and I admire you. Congratulations, and have no second thoughts about me. I shall always be your friend." (And, as a matter of fact, he was.) I was profoundly touched by his generous attitude.

(I did not see Marc again until after the war, for he had been taken prisoner. When he returned, Widor and I persuaded him to compete again for the Grand Prix de Rome, and we had the great joy of seeing him finally win.)

The day after the competition, Widor asked me to play for Vespers at Saint-Sulpice. Saint-Saëns attended, for the choir was scheduled to sing some of his motets during the service. Knowing he was there, I played his Prelude and Fugue in E-flat for the postlude. Afterward, Widor said to me, "Monday afternoon, you should visit Saint-Saëns at his apartment in the rue de Courcelles. Thank him for your *prix*. Furthermore, he wishes to know you better." I assured Widor that I would go.

60

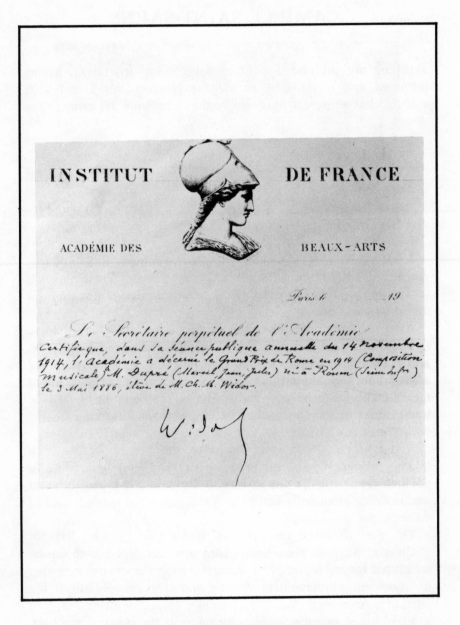

Fig. 23 — Certificate, Grand Prix de Rome.

CAMILLE SAINT-SAËNS

Keeping my promise, I went to Saint-Saëns' apartment, having prepared and memorized an elegant greeting, for I had been warned that this great musician could be brusque. He came to the door.

"What do you wish?" he said curtly.
"Maître, I am here to thank you for your kind. . ." No time for my fine phrases.
"Now I remember. . . kindness, nothing of the sort. I voted for you because you deserved it. You have nothing to thank me for."

I felt encouraged, for so far, things were going well. Saint-Saëns continued, "I read your biography in this morning's newspaper. Is it true you were a child prodigy?" I remained silent. "But why not admit it? I was one also."

From this moment forward he was charming and interesting, and as I started to leave, he said, "Please stay a while." He kept me a long time, speaking of Rouen, of the organ at Saint-Ouen, and of Cavaillé-Coll, whom he greatly admired. Mostly he talked of keyboard technique and of orchestration. When I did leave finally, I was "in seventh heaven."

The following year, on New Year's Day to be exact, Widor advised me to visit Saint-Saëns again, to extend in person my best wishes for the coming year. "He asked about you recently and he wants to see you again."

Clearly, he had completely forgotten his invitation, for he welcomed me cooly:
"Monsieur, tell me quickly what you want. I am very busy!"

I had heard many stories about his capricious moods, and for a moment I was bewildered. Then, collecting myself, I said, "Maître, I do not want anything. I came to see you to extend to you in person my greetings for the New Year."

"You came to see me, and not to solicit a favor? That is rare! Yes, yes, now I remember. . .Rouen, Saint-Ouen, Cavaillé-Coll. ."

Then he began to talk about music, especially singing — about famous coloraturas of the past who dared to introduce their own variations in Rossini's songs. Seating himself at the piano, he continued, "Here is the song as Rossini wrote it — and here is what Madame La Patti, Madame Viardot, and others did to it." All the examples were in his fingers.

Finally, taking advantage of a pause in the music, I acquired some courage and asked him to tell me about his friend Liszt. "You like Liszt? Good for you! Here is one of my favorite recollections of him. Liszt was not only a very great musician, but he was also a very wonderful man. He knew how to put one at ease with just a few kind words. I myself experienced this trait the first time he asked me to play. He wanted me to sight read at the piano an orchestral score with him. As I stood shaking, Liszt said quietly, 'You will see, everything will be fine. You have nothing to worry about. I know you sight read very well. This is how we shall do it: I shall take the lower parts and work the pedal while you will take the upper parts and turn the pages. In this way you will have only *some* of the instrumental parts. I shall take the others. Things will go together, you will see!' And he always informed me in advance of his trips to Paris. Before his arrival I would go to all the Parisian publishers, who were kind enough to lend me the most recent orchestral scores. Liszt and I sight read them together in my apartment, rue Monsieur-le-Prince. For me these were marvelous and unforgettable hours."

After my visit I saw Saint-Saëns again at the celebration of his jubilee. For the event an orchestra organized by the Société des Concerts performed The Deluge and his Third Symphony, with Saint-Saëns himself at the organ for the latter. When the committee-in-charge asked him which one of his concertos he wished to perform, he replied, "Since you are giving this concert to please me, permit me to play not one of mine, but Mozart's Concerto in D minor. I have always wanted to play this piece." It goes without saying that the committee agreed to his wish, and he was brilliant.

Fig. 24 — Camille Saint-Saëns at the organ.

A fond memory of this program stays with me. Saint-Saëns, who, as I said, played the organ part in his Third Symphony, asked me to turn pages for him. So I followed him up the steep little staircase leading to the organ console. After the performance of this work, as we started to go down the steps, Saint-Saëns faltered. I timidly offered my help, which he spontaneously accepted. We descended slowly — I in front, he behind, his hand on my shoulder. "Safe and sound," he said merrily as we arrived at the foot of the stairs. What a precious photo I could have had for my souvenir album!

I saw him once more, several months before his death, at a concert which took place at the Institut. His Septet for trumpet, strings and piano was performed, he himself playing the piano part. As I arrived for the program, I noticed Saint-Saëns in front of me, walking slowly. I hesitated. He was joined a moment later by a member of the Académie des Sciences, a man equal in age, and I overheard this little conversation:

"Now then, Monsieur Saint-Saëns, our old legs do not function so well any longer."
Saint-Saëns replied furiously, "That is right, our legs do not. But in a few minutes you will see how my fingers function!"
As a matter of fact, his fingers proved to be still very much in form. He was a great success.

Several years later I had a strange encounter. During a taxi ride from my house to the train station, the driver asked, "Excuse me, are you not Monsieur Marcel Dupré?" I was, for a long time, a butler for Monsieur Saint-Saëns, and I can remember the day when you came to see him, just after winning your Grand Prix de Rome. I also remember an evening when a Monsieur Paul Dukas came. After dinner these gentlemen sat at the piano. On the music rack was a large manuscript on which was hand-printed in large letters *The Sorcerer's Apprentice (L'Apprenti Sorcier)*. When Monsieur Saint-Saëns dismissed me for the evening, I retired. To my astonishment, the next morning I found them still at the piano having a great discussion."

I often think about this scene. It would be interesting to know the outcome!

WAR, 1914

I had been disqualified for military service because of the operation on my right collar bone. But as soon as mobilization began, I went to a military doctor I knew in Rouen; I wanted my status changed. He told me to wait, as he felt there would soon be a revision of the regulations. "However, in the meantime, since you want to join the war effort, go to Saint-Gervais' Hospital. See what you can do there to help." I took his advice. Unfortunately, I was again invalidated for military service, even under the revised regulations, so I stayed at the hospital, working in the pharmacy for two years. Then in October 1916 the hospital was reorganized, and I was relieved of my duties, but not without a wonderful letter of appreciation.

Many of my friends were killed in the war. Grieved, I decided to compose a *De Profundis* in memory of all the wartime dead. I began to write, and in my work I found a sense of consolation.

During this same month of October 1916, Louis Vierne, organist of Notre-Dame Cathedral, left for Lausanne to receive special treatment for his eyes. He asked me to substitute at Notre-Dame for five months. These five months turned into five years.

Just after the war had finished, Cardinal Amette sent for me one Sunday. "Have you read the newspapers this morning? They announced the reopening of the Villa Medicis in Rome. Are you going to leave us?" [All Prix de Rome laureates were required to spend four years in Rome composing. The sojourn was financed by the French government.] Taken by surprise, I replied that I would consult Widor, Secrétaire Perpétuel of the Académie, and I would try to come back to see him that very afternoon. Widor's answer came quickly.

"You should not abandon Notre-Dame to go to the Villa Medicis to 'muse' for four years. You must have the courage to

give up this Roman sojourn. You are thirty-three years old, and it is time for you to concentrate on your concert career."

"But what will the Académie say?"

"Your required compositions, are they finished?" (It was necessary, during the sojourn in Rome, to submit a musical work to the Académie each year.)

"Yes, all of them," I replied.

"Bring them to me tomorrow. We shall write a letter to the Académie asking for a decision in this matter. In the meanwhile, tell the Cardinal that you will remain in your post at Notre-Dame."

Widor read our letter at the next meeting. My lot was decided in accordance with an old rule (still valid at the time) which required all recipients of the Grand Prix de Rome to spend two years in Rome, but which allowed them to reside for the remaining two years in any European city, Paris included. My two years in Rome were waived, the equivalent of two years in Paris was financed, and an important chapter in my life was finished. The Villa Medicis was a so-called "Paradise Lost" for me; but I went to visit it a few years later on the occasion of my first concert in Rome.

Fig. 25 — Marcel Dupré at Notre-Dame.

GREAT BRITAIN

CLAUDE JOHNSON

It was at Notre-Dame that I had one of the great strokes of good luck of my career.

Two days after the Feast of the Assumption in 1919, I received a letter from an Englishman. "I was present on the fifteenth of August for Vespers at Notre-Dame. After the service I went to the sacristy to ask who the organist was and what pieces he had played. They told me that the organist was Marcel Dupré, and that he had probably improvised between each of the versets at Vespers. If these pieces are published, where can I find them? If they were improvised, would you be able to compose ten similar pieces for me? I am offering you the sum of fifteen hundred francs. I shall have them published in London by Novello and Co. Ltd., but you will retain control of the copyright."

I felt as if my head were spinning. My correspondant was none other than Claude Johnson, one of the directors of Rolls-Royce.

I replied immediately, accepting his offer with gratitude, and at the same time, I confirmed the fact that he had indeed heard improvisations. I explained that I would be unable, obviously, to guarantee an exact reproduction of them, but that I would try to re-establish the same mood. In conclusion, I added that, in place of ten versets, I would write fifteen, for the Office of the Feast of the Virgin Mary had fifteen musical interludes. Even before I began to compose the pieces, he sent me a check, adding five hundred francs to aid the work of the cathedral choir.

The fifteen pieces were composed quickly; and when Claude Johnson returned from a trip to the United States, he stopped in Rouen. There I played the versets for him on the magnificent Cavaillé-Coll at Saint-Ouen. The next day I played them for him on the organ at Notre-Dame, where he became a frequent visitor in the organ loft.

One Sunday when he was present, while I was playing full organ, the wind supply stopped suddenly. (In those years the organist was at the mercy of a team of five men who would stop pumping wind whenever they became tired. So I was always careful not to use too much wind.) "What is the matter?" asked Johnson. I explained the sitution. "Wait a minute, I am going to talk with them." He returned beaming. "I gave them some money. Everything will be just fine now." I thought that it would have been wiser perhaps to wait until I had finished playing before being so generous. I started to play again and there was another stoppage. "Things can not go on like this! . . . I would like to give an electric blower to Notre-Dame. Would you ask the firm of Cavaillé-Coll to draw up a plan? Since I am an Anglican, it would probably be wise to have the cardinal's consent for this project." I went to find Cardinal Dubois, and he promptly agreed to it. So, after many centuries, Notre-Dame was going to have her first electric blower.

This was not the last good deed of this generous man. "You have never been to England," he said to me one day. "I have thought about the idea of organizing a concert in London at Royal Albert Hall, under the patronage of the Prince of Wales (the future Edward VIII). I will engage a choral group, and the English public will hear the pieces I commissioned. We shall intersperse the organ pieces with the choral versets, as at Notre-Dame. Naturally, the program will also include other compositions of your choice. Rest assured that if your name is not yet known in England, it will be! And you will have a large following. My friend Lord Northcliffe, owner of several daily newspapers, will provide publicity." I never even dreamed of such a start in England!

The concert took place on the ninth of December, 1920, in the presence of a full house of some nine thousand people. My whole family had been invited, and our trip to London and our stay there was like a fairy tale: a Rolls-Royce came to Rouen for us, a sumptuous apartment was reserved for us in London, and even a secretary was at our disposal.

At the concert the choir was outstanding. I myself received a very moving ovation. The happiest of all, I believe, was my very dear Claude Johnson. After the concert I was presented to the Prince of Wales.

My concert tours of Great Britain began shortly thereafter and continued for thirty-five years.

Fig. 26 — Marcel Dupré, Claude Johnson and Lynwood Farnam.

SIR HENRY WOOD

Several wonderful memories come to mind. Mostly, I think of the Promenade Concerts at Queen's Hall (destroyed during World War II), a series started by Sir Henry — concerts he directed for forty years. He often invited me to participate in these very popular concerts, which took place every evening except Sunday during the months of August and September.

From the windows of our hotel just opposite the hall, we would see people begin to gather before the locked doors by five o'clock. Many would buy tickets for the parquet, a favorite area in the middle of the hall. There everyone stood throughout the concert, packed against each other. Blocks of ice placed on platforms at the foot of the stage helped to keep the hall cool. At the rear of the stage, and high above it, stood the large organ.

Sir Henry's entrance, a white carnation in his lapel, was always accompanied by tumultuous applause. The atmosphere at these concerts was exciting, and I always enjoyed playing for such a very attentive and enthusiastic audience. Sir Henry conducted his orchestra with a dash, a warmth and an enthusiasm that electrified his listeners. His programs were very eclectic. He performed much French music; and it was in Queen's Hall that Sir Henry conducted the première of my Symphony for organ and orchestra.

The one hundredth anniversary of his birth was celebrated in 1969, and the BBC came to Meudon to interview me, to record for broadcast my homage to this great man.

Another wonderful memory comes from my association with Sir Henry. After one of our concerts, in which he had accompanied me in Handel's Concerto in D minor for organ and orchestra, a work he was especially fond of, he said to me, "I wish, at any price, to engage you for the Handel Festival at the Crystal Palace." (This building was completely destroyed by fire on the thirtieth of November, 1936.)

This festival took place every three years, and one had to be a British subject to participate in it. "I have an idea," Sir Henry said to me, "I shall explain to the authorities that I would love to re-establish, with you as organist, Handel's custom of improvising cadenzas in his organ concertos at those spots marked *ad libitum* in his manuscripts." His plan was approved.

These festivals had a grandiose character: an orchestra of five hundred musicians, including four hundred strings; a choir of four hundred voices; a large organ; twenty thousand listeners; and the patronage of King George V and Queen Mary. "Above all, no encores in the presence of the sovereigns," he advised me, "but you may take as many bows as you wish." I took nine! Yet, it was not my success which remains embedded in my memory. It is what I heard next. As soon as I had finished playing, my impresario came looking for me. He wished to hear Handel's "Hallelujah" chorus from the back of the hall and had reserved two seats. He gave me his other ticket. The sound of the four hundred voices and this huge orchestra was so splendid that I felt I was in another world. After the last "Hallelujah" thundered toward the skies, I was standing with the crowd, tears running down my cheeks.

WESTMINSTER CATHEDRAL AND CARDINAL BOURNE

Another wonderful memory from my tours in Great Britain comes from one of my many recitals in Westminster Cathedral. The great organ builder Henry Willis, who was one of my closest friends, had just built an organ for the cathedral. He suggested to Cardinal Bourne that I be invited to play the opening recital. The cardinal extended the invitation, and it was on this inaugural program, the ninth of October 1925, that I gave the first performance of my *Symphonie-Passion*.

On the day of the recital I offered to play for the high mass. As I approached the organ loft I found myself face to face with Cardinal Bourne. He was at his priedieu, following the service unobserved. He said in excellent French, "The boy choir is going to sing a motet by Palestrina during the Offertory. May I join you in the organ loft and have your impressions?" During their singing I felt his eyes upon me, looking for my reactions, and I was glad to be able to tell him, in all sincerity, that the choir was superb, having perfect intonation and a wonderfully pure sound.

He invited me to lunch the next day. First he talked about the time we met in Lisieux in 1923 (he had officiated and I had played at ceremonies celebrating the beatification of Sister Thérèse). Then he spoke of his youth, when he studied at the Seminary of Saint-Sulpice in Paris. Finally he mentioned the ceremony in Rouen in 1931 commemorating the five hundredth anniversary of the burning of Jeanne d'Arc. He had been sent to the celebration as a papal legate. He remembered well the occasion. At one point he said: "The English were horrible in their treatment of Jeanne d'Arc," then he added, with a sly smile, "but so were the French."

My recitals at Westminster Cathedral, usually attended by large crowds, always gave me much satisfaction. My dear Claude Johnson was always present, and we usually ended the evening together. A close friendship developed between us. He was an intelligent, kind and gentle man. Each year we were invited to spend part of our summer vacation at his Kingsdown estate, the Villa Vita, situated on a cliff not far from Dover. (In good weather we were able to see the coast of France — Cape Griz-Nez.) When we arrived, our eyes were drawn first of all to an immense French flag flown in our honor. This was always a thrilling moment. He died at the age of sixty, leaving a great emptiness in our lives, but many unforgettable memories as well.

LORD GLENTANAR

In September of 1927 I made the very long trip from Paris to northern Scotland to play a single concert! Yet, I have never regretted it. I had been invited by Lord Glentanar to play the inaugural recital on his residence organ.

One morning I arrived at a little train station north of Aberdeen where a limousine was waiting for me. After several minutes' drive we entered a park through which we continued for more than half an hour: valleys, hills, streams, one after the other. Finally Lord Glentanar's enormous manor house appeared.

My host gave me a warm welcome. I was surprised by his youth and even more surprised by a music room with more than four hundred seats. There was a stage, set up with enough music stands for an entire symphony orchestra. At the back of the stage stood a four-manual organ of eighty stops. Lord Glentanar told me that he adored music, confinding that he had studied it seriously in his youth — piano, organ, harmony, fugue, orchestration and conducting.

On the program he had interspersed my organ solos with several orchestral works. I remember the overture to *Die Meistersinger*, which he himself conducted quite remarkably. He had engaged the same fine orchestra from Edinburgh that he brought frequently to his home.

The next day, after touring his marvelous estate, I was driven back to the little station. Lord Glentanar had arranged to have an express train make an unscheduled stop in order to pick me up for my return to London.

MY BACH RECITALS

The year was 1920, the same year as my London debut. The war was over, and my dream of playing the complete organ works of Bach from memory again filled my mind. I began to work seriously on the project. But where could I present this series of recitals? Fortune came to the rescue!

One day I ran into Cortot. He told me he wished to hear the organ at Notre-Dame. We decided to meet there one evening. It was at that time of year when the days are very long. The sun still illuminated the rose window at the west end of the cathedral, and the entire edifice was bathed in a warm glow. Cortot asked me to play some Bach and I took the occasion to tell him of my project. He was enthusiastic about it.

"Where will you give them? Here at Notre-Dame?"
"No, that is impossible. I am only the interim organist here."
"At the Trocadéro?"
"That hall would be ideal, but my financial means will not permit me to take such a risk. It would be costly to rent the Trocadéro for ten recitals. I simply thought about using the small hall at the Conservatoire."
"On that little organ?" (It is somewhat larger now.)
"Why not, it is possible."
"Have you thought about this carefully? . . . All right, I will help you."

Forty-eight hours later he telephoned me. "Any time after tomorrow, go thank Paul Léon, directeur des Beaux-Arts,* who consented to let you use the hall at the Conservatoire. You should also thank Fauré, the director of the Conservatoire, and Gigout,

*Association française d'Expansion et d'Échanges artistiques avec l'étranger, sous les auspices du Ministère de l'Instruction publique et des Beaux-Arts. This governmental agency for the promotion of the arts is not to be confused with the Académie des Beaux-Arts.

the professor of organ." Thus, Cortot had arranged everything.

To prepare for these recitals I went to the Conservatoire each evening to practice from eight o'clock until midnight. One evening the custodian entered, carrying a plate with two appetizing eggs on it. "You work too hard, like a demon. You forget to eat. Here are two eggs fresh from our chicken coop." I was deeply touched by his thoughtfulness, promising him that I would take better care of myself.

My programs were given on Friday evenings during the first three months of the year 1920. The little hall and the stage were always packed, and this was a great encouragement for me. I can remember an amusing detail: invited officials, teachers at the Conservatoire, members of the Institut (all of them sitting in choice seats) offered, one by one, their seats to ladies, while they themselves had to sit on the steps leading to the stage.

I have rarely found such a congenial atmosphere. I could sense the fervor with which everyone listened to Bach's divine music. At the last program Widor spoke briefly, and I was very touched when he concluded, "Rest assured, if Bach had been here, he would have pressed you to his heart."

The next morning I went to rehearse my Fantasy for piano and orchestra, which was to be performed the following day at the Concerts Lamoureux, with Pierné conducting. After this concert I had several days of well-earned rest in the south of France.

The following year, I was able to realize my dream of playing my ten Bach programs on the wonderful organ in the hall at the Trocadéro.

Fig. 27 — Former organ, Paris Conservatoire

AMERICA

A short while after my first concert in London I received a visit from an American, Dr. Alexander Russell, a former pupil of Widor. He was director of music for the John Wanamaker Stores in New York and Philadelphia. "My employer, Mr. Rodman Wanamaker, a great lover of music, recently bought an organ of 145 stops which had been constructed for the Saint Louis Exposition, and which was inaugurated by your maître Alexandre Guilmant."

Before revealing to me the reason for his visit, Dr. Russell told me about this instrument. After the exposition the organ was to have been purchased by the municipality of Saint Louis for the auditorium in the City Hall. Instead, it was placed in the hands of an organ building firm for resale. This firm, on the verge of bankruptcy, had been unable to find a buyer for the organ. Mr. Wanamaker, when he learned of the situation, decided to buy not only the organ, but the entire firm and all of its material. The workers moved to Philadelphia, and an entire floor in the John Wanamaker Store was turned into an organ factory. Mr. Wanamaker had the organ enlarged from 145 stops to 234. Then he had another organ of 117 stops built for the concert hall in his New York store. When this second instrument was completed, Dr. Russell was sent to Europe to engage a young organist, preferably French, to inaugurate the New York organ with a series of twelve recitals, and to play, afterward, six programs on the Philadelphia organ. "I went to see Widor," Dr. Russell said, "and he sent me to see you. If you agree to come to the United States under our exclusive management, the following year we will organize a hundred concerts for you throughout the country." Russell's proposal, like Claude Johnson's, left me speechless. Although somewhat skeptical about the second half of the proposal, I accepted, naturally.

Because of a stupid accident in which I had hurt one of my

Fig. 28 — Marcel Dupré in America

fingers, I was unable to play for Dr. Russell. When he returned to New York, he was obliged to give Mr. Wanamaker the whole truth concerning his negotiations with me. "You engaged Marcel Dupré simply on the strength of Widor's opinion? You yourself did not hear him play? Well ... I am sure we can have complete confidence in Widor!" Dr. Russell told me some time later how relieved he was to hear Mr. Wanamaker's last sentence!

In November 1921 I made my first Atlantic crossing, and as soon as I arrived in New York I played for Mr. Wanamaker himself.

I submitted my eighteen programs to Dr. Russell, placing an improvised four-movement organ symphony on the last New York recital. "That will not do," he said to me. "It is not on the last program but on the first one that you must put this symphony. The press as well as all the leading New York organists will be there." I hesitated, for this was to be my first experience in public with this type of improvisation. But in the end I followed his advice. I was given excellent themes by several organists who were present,* and I was fortunate that one of the leading New York

Fig. 29 — Dupré at the Wanamaker organ in New York

*Those organists who submitted themes for the improvisation were: Edward Shippen Barnes, Charles M. Courboin, Clarence Dickinson, Lynwood Farnam, T. Tertius Noble and Frederick Schlieder.

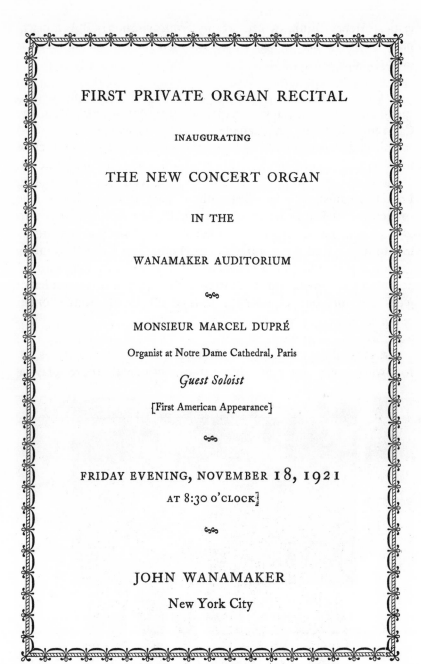

Fig. 30 — Program: Dupré's first American appearance

critics, Henry Fink, wrote of my improvisation: "A musical miracle." "We did it!" exclaimed a radiant Dr. Russell. "Success is ours throughout America."

Around Christmas I had a free week which I had planned to spend in New York. I was surprised to receive a letter from the Casavant brothers in Canada, French Canadians who had established an organ building firm in Saint-Hyacinthe, a town close to Montreal. I had already heard about their fine instruments. Their letter was worded as follows: "We can not let a young French organist visit America without hearing his native tongue spoken in Quebec Province! Consequently, we are inviting you to spend Christmas week with us. First we shall show you our organs in Montreal, then you will visit our factory in Saint-Hyacinthe. Enclosed you will find a check to cover your travel expenses." I accepted the invitation enthusiastically. This was a wonderful week for me, one in which I learned all about electric organ actions.

Dr. Russell kept his promise. I returned to the United States the following year for my first transcontinental tour, playing

Fig. 31 — Edouard Monet, Lanquetuit, Marcel and Albert Dupré,
Dr. Alexander Russell

Fig. 32 — Laberge, Dupré and family, and Farnam in Rouen

ninety-four concerts. I was well received everywhere.

It was with the cooperation of Dr. Russell and the impresario Bernard Laberge, a French Canadian living in New York, that this concert tour and the following ones were arranged. "Next year," Dr. Russell said to me, "I want you to give a hundred concerts, like Paderewski." I played a hundred and ten in six months, and I returned to France somewhat thinner!

In 1924 my close Belgian friend Charles Courboin (who became organist at both St. Patrick's Cathedral in New York City and the John Wanamaker Store in Philadelphia) and I gave a joint concert in the Philadelphia store, the Philadelphia Orchestra, conducted by Stokowski, participating. The program concluded with Wagner's famous "Ride of the Walkyries." Russell came looking for me. "We are going up to the eighth floor of the Grand Court. From there the sound of the organ and orchestra will be extraordinary." We went, and as I stood and listened, I saw Rodman Wanamaker himself standing in a corner. (It was his practice to circulate through his stores. Since he had never allowed himself to be

Fig. 33 — Bossi, Nadia Boulanger, Courboin and Dupré in Philadelphia

photographed, his employees did not recognize him.) When the concert was finished, we went up to him. "Come with Courboin to see me tomorrow in my New York office," he said. "I want to tell you about several ideas which came to mind during the concert." The next day we went to see him.

"I have decided to enlarge the organ in my Philadelphia store. Work together to draw up a plan for the instrument. Use everything you ever dreamed about."

Courboin asked, "How much space do we have at our disposal?"

Wanamaker replied, "The organ presently occupies two floors; you have six left!"

And I asked naïvely, "And what about the budget?"

"No limit, Dupré." With no limit, we had all sorts of possibilities.

This project decided upon, Mr. Wanamaker continued, "The musicians in the Philadelphia Orchestra are all virtuosos. But they do not have instruments which equal their talents. How would the orchestra sound if the violinists, the cellists and the violists had in their hands some old instruments of Stradivarius, Guarnerius, Amati, etc.?" And without waiting for our answer he said to Dr. Russell, "Go to Europe next summer and start a collection of Italian string instruments. I would like sixty of them."

Mr. Wanamaker saw his dreams realized. The organ, enlarged from 234 stops to 451, was controlled from a new six-manual console. And the string collection was assembled in two years. (I have played with those marvelous strings whose sonority was most beautiful.) Alas, Mr. Wanamaker died three years later, at the age of sixty-five, and the collection of old instruments was split up by his inheritors. His death also marked the end of the magnificent concerts in his stores.

The organization of these concerts was remarkable. After the store closed an "army" of workers arrived. The counters and display cases disappeared, seats were set up everywhere, and a printed program was placed upon each chair. (The concerts were by invitation only; however, all an individual had to do to receive one was to send his name, address, and telephone number to the store. Each family was allowed two seats.) Sometimes there were as many as several thousand listeners.

I shall never forget the evening of the eighth of December, 1921, when, having been given several themes — 'Jesus, Redemptor.' 'Adeste fidelis,' 'Stabat Mater' and 'Adoro te' — I decided, in a flash, to improvise an organ symphony in four movements which depicted in music the life of Jesus: "The world awaiting the Saviour," "Nativity," "Crucifixion" and "Resurrection." This improvisation was to become my *Symphonie-Passion,* a work I began to compose when I returned to France. As Dr. Russell announced my scheme to the audience, everyone in the Grand Court stood up. Encouraged by this enthusiasm, I improvised, feeling as I had never felt before.

The frequency of my concert tours in America had to change when I was placed in charge of the organ class at the Conservatoire in 1926. I could not be absent for long periods of time. It was decided that I could make a three-month concert tour every three years.

Unfortunately, too many concerts were scheduled during this short period, and these tours were exhausting. I had no time to relax. I was "caught in the trap," so to speak, as soon as I arrived in New York. When the boat docked, both journalists and photographers were waiting for me. Then, at the hotel in each city, there were interviews. Frequently the most unexpected and amusing questions were asked. "It seems that you have worn the same hat since you first came to America." (I suppose this was a polite way of saying, "Where did you ever get that hat?" It never occurred to me that my rather large-brimmed black hat would seem unusual to Americans!) Or another: "With what shoes do you play the organ pedals?" A bit puzzled, I replied, "With my own!"

In California, someone asked, "What do you think of Clemenceau?" I answered briefly, "He played an important part in the war." The next day I was astonished to read a headline in the local newspaper: "Clemenceau's policies supported by Marcel Dupré." I learned to be more careful about my comments.

I would have liked to have had the time to stop here and there, to see, as they say, a little of America. It was not until the sixth tour that I was able, finally, to admire Niagara Falls, even though I had previously given several concerts in that area. And on the next to the last tour, a break in my schedule, thanks to the Christmas holidays, permitted a visit to the Grand Canyon. What an extraordinary sight, especially at sunrise!

Finally in 1948, having crisscrossed American many times (much of our travel was done at night in order to reach the next destination for a concert the following day), my wife and I decided that this tour, the tenth one, would be the last. And we stood fast by our decision, resisting many requests to tour in America again.

I did, however, return to the United Sates two more times, for just a few days each time — to Detroit.* The first trip was made in response to an invitation from my close friend Paul Paray, who had asked me to inaugurate the organ in the Ford Auditorium. "I forbid you to say 'no'," he wrote. The second visit was made at the invitation of a former, very dear pupil, Frederick Marriott, who wanted me to inaugurate the new organ in the church where he was organist.

This last program was my final "adieu" to America. But my contacts with this great country continue. I meet many young American organists who come to visit me at Saint-Sulpice and in Meudon. I constantly receive programs which include my compositions. Every year my birthday is observed somewhere by a recital devoted to my music. These marks of esteem touch me deeply. I also have the joy of seeing our great French organists, most of them former pupils of mine, welcomed in America as I was. Thus they continue to hold aloft the torch first carried there by Alexandre Guilmant.

Although Dupré does not mention the fact, he also stopped on one of these trips in New York City in order to give a recital at St. Thomas Church, where he also made several recordings.

Fig. 34 – Marcel Dupré at the six-manual Wanamaker organ in Philadelphia

SWITZERLAND

My first concert tour in Switzerland was arranged by Cortot. He asked Robert Brussel, Léon's predecessor as the directeur des Beaux-Arts, to organize it. The latter sent for me one day. "Cortot wants you to make your debut in Switzerland. We have a budget of ten thousand francs. We shall schedule ten recitals and make all the arrangements." Several days before my departure I learned that this budget had been reduced to four thousand francs. I immediately contacted Brussel.

"Since the budget has been reduced, I shall play only four concerts. Is that not correct?"

"Not at all. The ten concerts are already organized." So I left for Switzerland, feeling somewhat discontented and a little anxious. Happily, the concerts were successful, and to my great surprise, I returned home with a profit. Quite proud, I hurried to the Beaux-Arts to give this money to Robert Brussel. "But, my dear friend, what do you want me to do with it? One does not return one's profits. I must think about it."

Some time later I was invited to a meeting to discuss a project of awarding grants to young talented musicians. [Dupré had donated these profits to help start the fund.] I found myself in the presence of a very select group, and seated myself timidly in the rear. I overheard a lady, the Duchess of X, ask her neighbor,

"Who is this young man?"

"His name is Marcel Dupré, and he has been to America, where he made millions!"

I was really amused. This so-called millionaire stepped down from his pedestal when, several minutes later, the amount of his contribution was announced!

PAUL HOEHN

Believing that I was completely unknown in Switzerland, I was pleasantly surprised to be met at the train station by a man I had seen several times in the organ loft at Notre-Dame. This individual, Paul Hoehn, was to become a second Claude Johnson for me. He was a marvelous friend whose precious guidance helped me to develop my career in Switzerland.

Paul, a great organ enthusiast, played the organ well, and he loved to substitute on Sundays in different churches. In his house he had a charming little organ. His home became my home whenever I was in Zurich, and I had some wonderful times there. He often went with me when I played recitals outside of Zurich — Lucerne, Basel, Winterthur, Bern, Saint-Gallen, Geneva, Neuchâtel, Lausanne, Montreux — helping me with many travel arrangements.

His death was a great loss. It was small consolation to be able to go to Zurich to play for his funeral, paying him my last homage with music that he loved.

I would not be able to close these pages on Switzerland without speaking about my dear pupil Heinrich Funk, organist at the Fraumünster in Zurich (I have often played in this church.) and a distinguished organ teacher at Zurich's Conservatory. To him goes my gratitude for his devotion to me.

THE BEATIFICATION OF SISTER THÉRÈSE OF LISIEUX

Three days of prayer in honor of the beatification of Sister Thérèse of the Infant Jesus ended with a ceremony on Wednesday, the eighth of August, 1923, in the Lisieux Cathedral. At the invitation of Monsignor Lemonnier, bishop of Bayeux, I had the honor of playing the organ. I began at eight-thirty in the morning and finished at ten-thirty in the evening, with only two interruptions.

During Vespers Cardinal Touchet, bishop of Orléans, gave a panegyric. He had been speaking for several minutes when I heard what sounded like a massive fluttering of wings. It was three thousand people turning a page at the same time! (The text of his remarks had been printed and distributed before the ceremony.) The cardinal, upset at this noisy intrusion, decided it was wiser to alter his text. (I had a similar experience: during my Bach recitals people followed the music, making noise in turning the pages. But I could not alter my music!) Skillfully he changed a word, then a sentence, and finally turned his entire presentation "inside out." (That evening, at a dinner party in the bishop's residence, Cardinal Touchet, mentioning the incident, confided to us what an unpleasant feeling he had experienced.)

After Vespers I went to the chapel of the Carmelite convent to play the organ for a ceremony during which the relics of Sister Thérèse were to be returned to their usual resting place. When it was finished, I climbed down the narrow staircase from the organ loft. When I was leaving, I found myself face to face with Cardinal Dubois, who had come, along with other prelates, to visit the convent. With a broad smile on his face, he said: "And what have you just been doing in a convent of cloistered nuns, Dupré?"

The final service took place in the cathedral after dinner. England was represented by Cardinal Bourne, archbishop of London, and the United States was represented by Cardinal Dougherthy, archbishop of Philadelphia. I improvised a postlude in which I used the themes of *God Save the King, The Star-spangled Banner, La Marseillaise* and César Franck's *Psalm CL,* an anthem which the choir had sung.

It was a most memorable day. When I returned home the following day, I found a letter waiting for me, informing me that I had been named a Chevalier de la Légion d'honneur. It was as if it were a wonderful "thank you" from that modest Norman nun, who was canonized two years later.

MEUDON

For a long time I had dreamed of buying a home in a suburb of Paris, a place where I could have a music room in which to work in peace. I asked an architect to look into the matter. Destiny willed that he would find a villa with some adjoining land in Meudon, only a few yards from the former residence of my late maître Guilmant. Several weeks after we had moved into our new home in 1925, I learned that the tenants of the Villa Guilmant were leaving and that Guilmant's organ was for sale. Even though my *salle d'orgue* was not yet finished and my plans for my residence organ were still incomplete, I could not ignore such an opportunity. I contacted Guilmant's granddaughter, Madame André Leblond, and her husband (both very good friends of mine), and I was able to conclude the transaction quickly. I was elated at the thought of having in my home the beautiful Cavaillé-Coll organ of my dear maître, an instrument which I had played so many times.

Fig. 35 — Marcel Dupré outside his home in Meudon

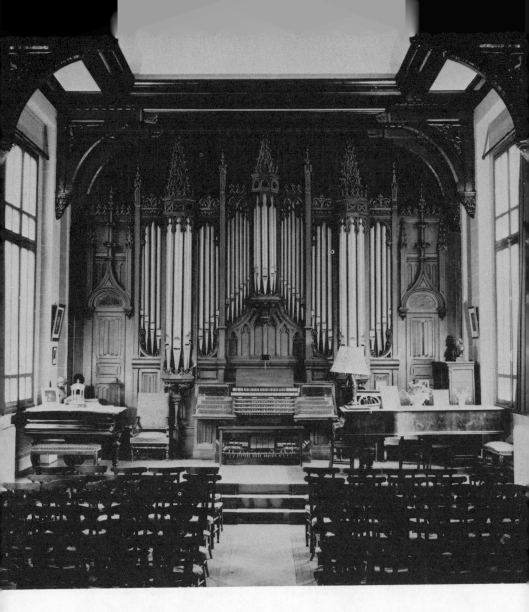

Fig. 36 — *Salle d'orgue*, Meudon

Other circumstances make my *salle d'orgue* very dear to me. After I had moved to Meudon, Claude Johnson, in what was to be his last generous gesture, sent me eight magnificient spandrels, wooden brackets of Scottish origin from a seventeenth-century hunting lodge of King Charles II. They support the ceiling and also provide splendid decoration. Alas, Claude Johnson died six months before its official opening. The evening of the inaugural recital, I opened the program with Bach's Passacaglia and Fugue, a work for which Johnson had a predilection, and one that I had often played for him.

Fig. 37 — Marcel Dupré exhibits the Guilmant console

THE ORGAN CLASS AT
THE CONSERVATOIRE

After the death of Eugène Gigout, organist of Saint-Augustin and professor of organ at the Conservatoire, Widor persuaded me that I should become a candidate to succeed him at the Conservatoire.

The competition was severe, for I had a formidable rival in the person of Charles Tournemire, organist of Sainte-Clotilde, who already taught a class in ensemble playing at the Conservatoire. On the day that I was planning to go to see Paul Léon at the Beaux-Arts, I learned just before I left home that some letters had been sent to members of the selection committee favoring my rival. Léon confirmed this news later in the day. He reassured me, "Do you not see that these letters will actually help you. The members of the committee do not like to be pressured into a choice. In fact, we have already taken a tally, and you should win on the first ballot with fifteen out of twenty-one votes." He was right; and I am forever grateful to Maurice Ravel, Paul Dukas, Gabriel Pierné and Alfred Bruneau, who campaigned, along with Widor, in my favor. Yet, the official signature of the Ministre des Affaires Culturelles took sixty days to obtain, during which time counter-proposals continued to be submitted. When the victory was mine finally, I went to thank Paul Léon. He said to me with a chuckle, "You *should* thank me! I have telephoned the Ministre almost every day to obtain his signature."

For twenty-eight years, from 1926 to 1954, this class was the center of my life. It was my passion and my joy, a joy enhanced by the brilliant careers of many of my former pupils.

A short time after my appointment, Gabriel Pierné, who had just conducted my Symphony for organ and orchestra at the Salle Gaveau, offered me the position of assistant conductor for the Concerts Colonne. I was extremely embarrassed to refuse him, but I did not feel at all qualified to fill this post. Widor again came to my rescue. He had a private conversation with Pierné, convincing him that it was wiser that I follow my career as an organist.

THE STATIONS OF THE CROSS

Apart from France, which I have crisscrossed in every direction, I have given concerts in other European countries: Germany, Austria, Switzerland, Italy, Spain, Holland and Belgium.

It was in Belgium that I had the idea for one of my major compositions, *The Stations of the Cross (Le Chemin de la Croix)*. A concert with a somewhat unusual format had been organized at the Brussels Conservatoire. For the first part of the program I played a short Bach recital on the beautiful Cavaillé-Coll organ. For the second part, Madame Madeleine Renaud, a professor at the Conservatoire, read a poem by Paul Claudel, *Le Chemin de la Croix*. I improvised a musical commentary on each station after it was read. It was during Lent, the thirteenth of February, 1931.

The audience's reaction was such that, the next day, on the train taking us back to Paris, my wife said,

"I have an idea."
"So do I," I replied.
"Speak up."
"No, you first."

In a word, I do not know which of us spoke first, but our ideas were exactly the same: that I should compose *The Stations of the Cross*, basing the movements on my improvisations. I started working, and the following year I gave the Paris première on the organ at the Trocadéro.

Fig. 38 — Manuscript: Page 1, Le Chemin de la Croix
Copyright 1932 by Durand et Cie. Copyright renewed.

THE TROCADÉRO ORGAN

The magnificent Cavaillé-Coll in the Trocadéro was very dear to me. Although the hall's acoustics were very poor for the spoken word and for orchestral music, they were superb for organ music. The instrument sounded splendid! (I knew the organ well, for while still a pupil of Guilmant, I had pulled stops for him during his series of historical organ recitals; and I myself had given numerous recitals on it.) But the time came when the organ needed a major restoration. I went to speak with Paul Léon, who had often exhibited an interest in my work. I gave him a full account of the poor condition of the organ. "If you were unknown to me, I would probably make up some vague excuse; but with you, I shall be quite frank. I am unable to raise the necessary funds at this time. I am indeed very sorry." I felt quite disappointed as I left his office.

A short time later, Frederick Mayer, one of my good American friends, organist of the Cadet Chapel at West Point (where he played a 200-stop organ), sent me a nice surprise — a check for five hundred dollars. It was in return for a small favor I had done for him. "During my last visit to Paris," he wrote, "I noticed that certain organs needed tuning and maintenance. Use this small sum of money as you see fit."

This last sentence gave me an idea. I went quickly to Widor and suggested that he head a committee to raise funds for the restoration of the Trocadéro organ, my five hundred dollars being a start. A committee was organized consisting of Widor, Bruneau, Pierné, my dear friend Edouard Monet (a second cousin of Claude Monet), the publisher Alphonse Leduc (as treasurer) and me. I returned, more boldly this time, to speak with Paul Léon, who could not conceal his satisfaction. He put me in touch with Monsieur Perchet, a supervisor of government buildings who later became chief architect for the government.

The firm of Cavaillé-Coll gave an estimate of sixty-six thousand francs for the necessary work. Thanks to several generous gifts we were able to raise thirty thousand francs quickly. The remainder resulted from public and private concerts that I gave. From Widor, on one side, and Monsieur Perchet, on the other, I received strong support.

One of my recitals for the benefit of the organ took place in 1926 at the Trocadéro itself. Widor, with tongue in cheek, addressed the audience: "Marcel Dupré, the man who asked me to plead before you the need to restore this noble instrument, is the worst champion of this cause. He conceals with such devilish ease all the organ's deficiencies that I risk being called a liar if I describe for you its pitiful state." With the proceeds from this last concert we reached the goal of our financial campaign; but someone informed me that we needed seventeen hundred francs more for some additional electrical wiring, an item none of us had even thought about.

"Can the state, which is getting the rebuilt organ as a gift, take care of this?" I asked Léon.
"Without a doubt, but only on next year's budget." Not wishing to delay the work, we raised the money ourselves, and the inaugural recital on this magnificently restored organ (not a single change had been made from the original design) took place on the second of March, 1927.

Alas, ten years later this masterpiece and the Trocadéro were both gone.* Before the demolition of the hall, I played the organ one last time for a group of my friends. Thinking all the while of its past, I played, with the sadness of a last farewell, the works that Franck, Guilmant and Widor had played for the original inauguration of the organ in 1878.

*The original pipe work was used by Victor and Fernando Gonzales in the eighty-stop organ they built for the Palais de Chaillot. They added a new console and various stops. The whole organ was mounted on a large wheeled platform, making it possible to move it to the best position for each program in which it was used.

Fig. 39 — Concert Hall, Trocadéro

MY CLASSES AT THE TROYES CONSERVATOIRE

In the course of my concert tours throughout France I had visited numerous regional conservatoires, and I saw for myself the deficiency in the teaching of certain subjects in a number of them. I thought a great deal about this problem.

One day my friend Amable Massis, director of the Troyes Conservatoire at the time, came to spend the day at Meudon. I questioned him about the curriculum, asking if he had, for example, a counterpoint class.

"My dear Marcel, you are dreaming. There is no money in the budget for this sort of thing."

"That is no obstacle. What would you say if I came to Troyes to teach every fifteen days?"

"But that is not possible," my wife exclaimed, "with all the work you have resting on your shoulders."

"You must know," I said to her, using my most persuasive tone of voice, "how important this matter is to me." In the end she resigned herself to my idea.

"What I have in mind," I explained, "is a five-year plan. There will be a class every week, but I shall teach it only every other week. Each time I come, I will bring you the lesson plan for the intervening class. That one *you* will teach. Together we shall cover harmony, counterpoint, fugue, analysis, composition and orchestration."

We began this project in 1935. Five years later, when fifth-year awards were presented, each student had orchestrated two pieces from an album of Grieg's piano pieces, and Amable Massis performed them with the school orchestra.

This was an exciting experiment — one finished just in time, for World War II was about to start.

After the war, in great part due to the efforts of Amable Massis, who had by then been appointed an Inspector-General for music, the instruction in regional Conservatoires improved immensely.

WORLD TOUR: AUSTRALIA AND NORTH AMERICA

The second of October, 1938, I gave a recital in London's Westminster Abbey. The director-general of Australia's radio network climbed up to the organ loft, coming to interview me after the concert. "You have already twice refused to come to Australia, using the pretext that you are a bad sailor. But the tropical seas are not the Atlantic! This time I shall not take 'no' for an answer. Besides, I have just invited Madame Dupré to come with you, and she seemed to like the idea."

In short, I let myself be convinced, and all the arrangements were made. Before our departure I was summoned by the Président de la République, Albert Lebrun. He informed me that he had just accorded the Légion d'honneur to the sister of Melbourne's mayor, for she had financed an edition of Couperin's works. He asked me to attend the official ceremony in Australia, expressing to her the gratitude of my country.

We embarked from Marseilles in June 1939 on board the S. S. Mooltan for a tour of twenty-five concerts — solo recitals and programs with orchestra — in the concert halls and the town halls of Sydney, Melbourne, Brisbane, and Hobart.

The twenty-three day crossing was excellent, so good, in fact, that I was able to work, making great strides in the preparation of my edition of Bach's organ works. I remember being quite amused when someone pointed out Mount Sinai in the distance, for at that very moment I was annotating the chorale "These are the Holy Ten Commandments." Our calls at the ports of Aden, Colombo, and especially Bombay, where we spent more time, were most interesting.

The sojourn of two months in Australia remains a wonderful memory for us. What a wonderful welcome I received — from the moment I played my first concert on the fine organ in Sydney's great Town Hall. (I had heard a great deal about this instrument,

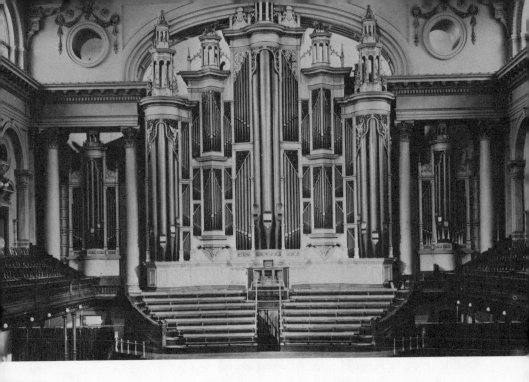

Fig. 40 – Organ, Town Hall, Sydney

which possessed a sixty-four-foot stop.) Fortunately, this tour was not like many of the others — no desperate races from city to city, nor from concert hall to train station. On this tour several concerts took place in the same locale, giving us time to become acquainted with the curious fauna of the area: kangaroos, koala bears, and in the immense forests, marvelous exotic birds, such as the lyrebird.

Unfortunately, the end of our stay was darkened by the threat of war. We left Sydney in a state of anxiety, and at Aukland, New Zealand, our first port of call, we had news of the Declaration of War. Many passengers left the ship to return immediately to Sydney.

The length of our stop over in Aukland was extended because of the arrest, on board, of a spy. (The captain had watched this man closely since our departure from Sydney.) The hours of waiting were somewhat less tense for us, because of the company of one of my former pupils, an Australian. He was the municipal organist in Aukland, and he took us to the Town Hall to hear the organ.

The twenty-one day trip continued across the Pacific. We were on our way to North America for a concert tour which had been organized for a long time. This trip would have been wonderful, very interesting, with ports of call in the Fiji and Hawaiian Islands, if it had not been for the uneasiness which gripped us. Since we had no additional news of the war, these weeks seemed interminable to us.

We disembarked at Vancouver, where the Canadian segment of my tour began. When we finally reached New York, we met our daughter Marguerite, who had joined us, not without a thousand difficulties, to participate as a pianist in several of my concerts.

Fig. 41 — Dupré inspects low C of the 64' Bombarde, Sydney

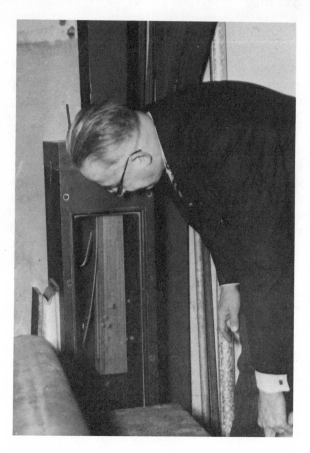

We left New York at the end of December on the last scheduled clipper flight to Europe. We were detained in Bermuda, the first refueling stop, for thirteen days, for the sea was too rough for the plane to take off. The passengers were lodged in a magnificent hotel. I began again to work, feverishly, on the preparation of my Bach edition. This intensive work helped to keep my mind off the war.

The first of January we read in the local newspaper that the Greek ship *Taxiarkus,* which was transporting our trunks to France, had sent out an S.O.S. What a miserable New Year's Day present! We resigned ourselves to the loss of everything. (Several months after our return home, we were informed that our trunks had miraculously reached Paris. They were a sorry-looking sight, for they had truly "sojourned" in the water; yet, there they were!)

On the evening of the thirteenth day we were able to leave Bermuda. We stopped next in the Azores. The sea was raging. No one was allowed to leave the aircraft, for it was necessary to take off as soon as possible. Three times the seaplane attempted a take off, only to snap back heavily into the sea. We were terrified. Finally, it was able to fly off. A stormy night, a dreadful crossing. Most of the night we were sick, and we arrived in Lisbon at dawn, thoroughly worn out.

One of our fellow-travellers, director of a Lisbon bank — we had made his acquaintance during our stopover in Bermuda — invited us to stay in his home. Since we were unable to leave for France until the next day — the Paris-Lisbon express was delayed because of flood waters — my host suggested that I give a recital that very evening in the Cathedral of Our Lady of Fatima. I was hardly in shape to play after such a trip, but I wanted to repay his kindness to us. Difficult as it was, I obliged. He asked the radio stations to announce the concert, and that evening there was a large crowd in the cathedral.

At last we left for France. In the train we had the pleasure to encounter Francis Poulenc and Pierre Bernac, who were going home after a concert tour of Portugal. After a brief stopover in Biarritz at my sister-in-law's home (her greeting of "our three heroes," gave us a good laugh), we were overjoyed to reach our dear Meudon.

WAR, 1940

We remained in Meudon during the entire Nazi occupation, living in a sort of solitude, the town being practically deserted. The first two Sundays, being deprived of all means of transportation, we walked to Saint-Sulpice.* Our fatigue was nothing compared to the joy we felt when we reached the organ, and I know that the parishioners still remaining in Paris found comfort when they heard it.

With the visit of some German officers who had come to inspect the area, our peace and quiet soon vanished — but, thanks be to God, not for long. They climbed to the roof of the *salle d'orgue.* From this spot one could see the whole city of Paris. They decided to install some anti-aircraft guns there, and for three days in a row they returned to plan the installation. At one point they came into the *salle d'orgue.*

"But it is a chapel!" exclaimed one officer.

"No," my wife answered, "it is a place where a musician works. If you place your guns on the roof, he will not be able to use the organ for his work."

"Yes, you are right. We shall think about it," replied the one officer who seemed to understand the situation.

We did not see them again, but we still remained a bit uneasy. Then one day we were amazed to see some workers on the roof of the neighboring villa. The tenant, an elderly lady, was being evicted. This poor woman arrived at our house in a state of shock. "Monsieur Dupré, I beg you, you are a famous man. Will you write to Hitler, asking him to let me remain in my house?" I would have laughed if the situation had not been so pathetic. We offered her a place in our home, but she refused, preferring to live in a small hotel.

This is a distance of several miles, and the Duprés were over fifty years old at the time.

After two weeks of working atop her villa, the Germans, for some unknown reason, began to dismantle everything, and they never attempted again to place antiaircraft guns in the vicinity.

But we experienced another upsetting incident during an air raid on the night of the third of March, 1942. A bomb that exploded nearby shattered all the windows in the house and made a shambles of the *salle d'orgue.*

When the raid was over we went downstairs to see the damage. The site was distressing. In the *salle d'orgue* the six large windows were broken, and the chairs and furniture in pieces. However, none of this really bothered us, for the organ was still there, miraculously intact. There was no electricity. But there was the magnificent moonlight to illuminate the organ case. We broke out in tears.

Fig. 42 — View of the *salle d'orgue* in Dupré's home
after a German bomb exploded nearby

The next morning I went to the Town Hall for help. I was told to contact a Monsieur Busigny who owned a large carpentry shop. He would be able to board up the windows. I contacted him, and that very afternoon some of his carpenters arrived. In twenty-four hours both the *salle d'orgue* and the house were protected from the elements.

When the workmen started to leave, I inquired,

"You are returning to Paris?"

"No, we are staying in Meudon, going now to our boss's house. It is as badly damaged as this one. But he himself said to us, 'Monsieur Dupré's organ comes first!' " I immediately went and offered my appreciation to this generous man. "Have you forgotten that charity well directed should begin *at home?*" At my question he started to laugh, the kind of laugh one hears when a practical joke is played.

The day after the Germans visited our house, I went to the Conservatoire to sit on a jury. We were to examine candidates in fugal composition. I found the building empty. Only one man, the treasurer, greeted me. "The examination is not being held," he said to me. "The director, Monsieur Rabaud, dismissed the candidates at two o'clock (they had been there since early morning), and he himself left for Bordeaux with some of the archives. I do not know what we should do. There are seven teachers and about twenty-five pupils still in Paris." The next day he telephoned me. "The Germans want to requisition the Conservatoire. If we reopen immediately, we can stop them! I have summoned all our teachers still in Paris." A faculty meeting took place. We decided to organize a small executive committee which would meet twice a week. We designated as chairman Louis Laloy, a remarkable musicologist. Next we distributed the teaching assignments, each of us having small classes.

The Conservatoire was passed over and left for us. One of our first tasks was to raise money for students who were without financial resources. To do this, we organized a concert which was held in the organ recital hall.

One day I was summoned by Monsieur Darras, Léon's

successor as directeur des Beaux-Arts. "As one of the individuals responsible for the Conservatoire," he said, "I am appointing you its temporary head. It is necessary to re-establish intellectual and artistic life in Paris, whatever the cost. Perhaps you could start by giving a concert at Saint-Sulpice for the benefit of pupils of the Conservatoire and the Académie des Beaux-Arts [School of Fine Arts]. In fact, I already have the support of the city's chief commissioner, the chancellor of the University, and Cardinal Suhard for such a program. The cardinal offered to be honorary chairman of the event. Surely you will want to go to thank him for his interest." His Eminence received me warmly. He had learned of my father's recent death in Biarritz — because of the war it was impossible for me to travel there — and his fatherly words eased a sorrowful heart. He occupied the place of honor at the concert and, with a crowded church, I was able to raise a sum of seventeen thousand francs for our cause.

WILHELM KEMPFF

After the hostilities ended, our friend Germaine Lubin, the incomparable interpreter of Wagner, came to visit us one day in Meudon. The great pianist Wilhelm Kempff was with her. We went into the *salle d'orgue,* and I improvised so that they could hear the different stops on the organ. Wilhelm Kempff, visibly interested, asked me several questions about the organ and its various stops and combinations. Then he asked my permission to play it. He sat down at the console and, in perfect style, played from memory Bach's Passacaglia and Fugue. I was pleasantly surprised. I thought I was entertaining a piano virtuoso, already famous, and I was discovering that Wilhelm Kempff was also a first-class organist. In talking about our families and our respective careers, I learned that he, like me, descended from a line of musicians, organists and choir directors, and that his parents had insisted on a rigorous musical education, just as mine had.

Fig. 43 — Marcel Dupré, about 1950

THE FIFTIETH ANNIVERSARY OF MY APPOINTMENT TO ROUEN'S CHURCH OF SAINT-VIVIEN

On the twenty-fifth of June, 1948, the fiftieth anniversary of my appointment as organist at Saint-Vivien was celebrated in my native city. In the afternoon I gave a recital on the organ upon which I started my career. It was very moving to find myself, after half a century, seated on that organ bench, in front of those three keyboards, just as in my youth. In remembrance I began my program with Bach's Prelude in E minor, the same piece I had played when I participated in Alexandre Guilmant's inaugural recital.

A great many friends were there. A number of my former pupils came from Paris and the various provinces. Some even came from foreign countries: Charles Hems (now deceased), teacher at the Brussels Conservatoire and organist of Sainte-Gudule; Heinrick Funk, a teacher at the Zurich Conservatory and organist at the Fraumünster; F. C. J. Swanton from Dublin, a concert organist and a true devotee of my music; Canon Delestre; and, of course, my very dear Marcel Lanquetuit, my first pupil (he was eight years old and I was fifteen), now organist at the Cathedral of Rouen.

The reception which followed at the Town Hall was indeed a wonderful gathering of friends.

That evening I gave a recital on the fine organ in the Church of Saint-Godard.

All these events were organized by the Comité Normand du Récital d'orgue, a group founded by André Renaudin. This committee, chaired by Madame Marie-Thérèse Simon, sponsors and organizes organ recitals in Normandy. Those given each year during August and September on the famous Cavaillé-Coll organ in Rouen's Saint-Ouen by great French and foreign organists attract a large and youthful public. I am happy to know that this series becomes more and more successful.

THE BACH YEAR

The year 1950 marked the two-hundredth anniversary of the death of Johann Sebastian Bach. I gave Bach recitals in various French towns and in foreign cities: London, Vienna, Munich, Hamburg, Lubeck, Luxembourg, Berlin and Luneburg.

There are two recollections in particular that are associated with the concerts in Germany. In Berlin, on a modern organ in the Martin Luther Church, I used some special echo effects in the Toccata and Fugue in D minor. My recital had been preceded by a noisy disturbance, for the church was too small to hold the large crowd trying to get in. The next day I learned from the newspaper that my registrations and my playing had produced an almost "meditative calm!" In Luneburg, on the famous organ dating from the great Cantor's time, an organ reverently preserved in Saint John's Church, I had the great honor of closing their series of Bach concerts.

ROME

The same year was also proclaimed a Holy Year. At the request of Count Vladimir d'Ormesson, ambassador to the Holy See, I was designated by the Académie des Beaux-Arts to go to Rome to give two concerts: one at the French Church of Saint-Louis, the other at the Pontifical Gregorian Institute.

When I arrived in Rome, I went to pay my respects to the French ambassador. He invited me to have lunch with him the next day. "After we have lunch," he said, "we shall attend a reception in your honor."

On the day of my program, as I arrived in the lobby of the Institute's concert hall, which had an organ of 125 stops, I was amazed to see Cardinal Tisserant waiting in the lobby. He said to me, smiling,

"Do you recognize me? I have changed since our meeting following your concert at Saint Catherine's Convent in Saint Paul, Minnesota. I have grown a beard, which, as you see, is now completely white."
"Your Eminence, look at my hair, which like your beard is beginning to go through the same 'transformation.' I have never forgotten those few hours that I had the honor to spend with you."

I was charmed by his conversation. He spoke primarily about the Vatican Library, where he was busy with the study of ancient texts, having made surprising discoveries about Latin authors with the aid of photography He added that he had intended to surprise me by presiding at this function.

After the program the ambassador informed me that at nine o'clock the next morning a courier would deliver an invitation for a private audience with the Pope at noon. At eleven-thirty I passed through the great bronze doors of the Vatican, surrounded by the

Swiss Guard in their red and yellow uniforms designed by Michelangelo. As soon as I had arrived in one of four large halls, the one for laity, Pius XII entered. He came up to me, "It is a pleasure to see a Frenchman. Of course I have heard about your concert last evening. How did you find the organ?" I did not lie in telling him that it was excellent. He blessed two medals for our twin granddaughters and after asking their first names, he said, "I bless these babies, their mother, your wife, and also your pupils who have consecrated themselves to religious music."

In October 1955 I was surprised to learn that I had been awarded a doctor's degree, *honoris causa*, by the Pontifical Gregorian Institute, and I was invited to come in November to receive my diploma. The ceremony took place in the hall where I had played in 1950. I received the parchment, beautifully hand-lettered in Latin, signed by Cardinal Pizzaro, who presented it to me.

After the ceremony Monsignor Ingles, the rector, asked my wife and me to be ready the next morning at ten o'clock. The Holy Father would receive us at eleven o'clock in Castelgandolfo.

On our arrival we noticed in the palace courtyard ten contrabass instrument cases arranged along a wall and an enormous truck with an inscription in big letters: Munich Symphony. Monsignor Ingles explained that the musicians had played in Rome the night before and had come, no doubt, to give a morning concert for the Pope.

There were about twenty people in the hall when the Pope arrived. An instant later a prelate entered and knelt before him, handing him a message. It was Monsignor Montini, pro-secretary of state, whom the Pope later named archbishop of Milan, the future Paul VI.

Pius XII remained among us for nearly forty minutes. Grouped around him, we listened to him speak simply and informally. "The musicians from Munich have just played a Mozart symphony for me," he said. "The 'Andante' was so beautiful that one might compare it to the music of angels."

Fig. 44 — Marcel Dupré receives a Doctor's Degree *(honoris causa)* from the Pontifical Gregorian Institute

DIRECTOR OF THE CONSERVATOIRE

Returning home from Nantes, where my friend Amable Massis had conducted a performance of my *De Profundis* at the Théâtre Graslin, I learned that the radio had just announced some terrible news: my old friend Claude Delvincourt was dead — killed that very day in an automobile accident on his way to Rome. I was stunned. I had dined with him only two evenings before at the Conservatoire. He had spoken of his trip to Rome to hear the first performance of his string quintet.

I was asked to succeed him as head of the Conservatoire. After much hesitation, I accepted, on the condition that I did not have to abandon my post at Saint-Sulpice and that I could continue to reside in Meudon. I was sixty-eight years old — only two years away from my retirement.

The two years as head of the Conservatoire were two difficult years, for I gave both body and soul to my post. I had the good fortune, however, to be assisted by a man with much experience and total devotion, Louis Chacaton. I cherish his memory.

After two years I regained my "freedom," being very happy to return to private life, to my organ, to my concertizing, to all my personal affairs.

In the meantime, in 1954, I had had the honor of being elected a member of the Académie, filling the place left vacant by Marcel Samuel-Rousseau. My election was formalized in a ceremony at the Conservatoire, marked by speeches by my close friends Paul Bazelaire and Alfred Cortot, and by the bestowal of the ceremonial sword, the beautiful work of the sculptor Lejeune.

LA FRANCE AU CALVAIRE

In 1945, seeing the horrible spectacle of Rouen devastated by war, I had the idea of writing a large-scale oratorio.

The year 1956 marked the five-hundredth anniversary of the retrial and the consequent restoration of Jeanne d'Arc's good name. Extensive plans were made to repair the severely damaged Rouen Cathedral so that it could be used for the celebrations.

I was asked to contribute to the event, so I set about finishing my oratorio *La France au Calvaire* for soloists, chorus, orchestra, and organ, based on a poem by my friend René Herval, who was also born in Rouen.

La France au Calvaire was performed for the first time on the twenty-fifth of June, 1956, under my direction. The chorus and orchestra of the Paris Conservatoire were augmented by a choir trained by my friend Elisabeth Brasseur. The soloists were Jacqueline Cellier, soprano; Jeannine Fourrier, contralto; Jean Giraudeau, tenor; and Xavier Depraz, bass. My pupil and friend of many years, Marcel Lanquetuit, was at the organ.

This recollection would be one of the most precious were it not linked in my memory to the death of my publisher Stéphane Bornemann. (I had close ties with him since the time he had agreed to publish my edition of the complete organ works of Bach.) He had accomplished a real tour de force, preparing on short notice, all the orchestral parts for my oratorio. Alas, he died in April, a few weeks before the first performance. His son, Maurice, however, had the great kindness to attend the performance in his late father's stead.

Fig. 45 — Medal honoring Dupré's eightieth birthday.

Fig. 46 — Marcel and Jeanne Dupré in Caen, 1957.

Fig. 47 – Organ console, Saint-Sulpice

OTHERS I REMEMBER

I would like to recall a few other great musicians who return to my thoughts from time to time. Unfortunately, I did not have any real contact with the two very great ones whom I admire: Debussy and Ravel.

CLAUDE DEBUSSY

I have a very sad recollection of Debussy. I met him toward the end of World War I at a benefit concert given by the great pianist Francis Planté. The concert was held in the crypt of Saint-Honoré d'Eylau. We had just taken our places when Debussy arrived accompanied by his wife. They sat just in front of us. Widor, who was with me, introduced me. I was startled by the look of suffering on Debussy's face. During the concert we saw him take a small syringe from his pocket, and he pricked his wrist with it. Then, at intermission, he excused himself and left, not feeling well. He died only a short time thereafter.

MAURICE RAVEL

My encounter with Ravel was brief yet important to me. I was with several friends in the courtyard of the old Conservatoire when suddenly I noticed Ravel leaving. He had been serving that day on a jury holding examinations. To my great surprise, he came straight towards me. "Set your mind at ease, Dupré. We are for you, and you will be elected." (I had posed my candidacy for the position of professor of organ.) He shook my hand warmly and disappeared. I stood still a moment, rooted to the spot, overwhelmed by his kindness and graciousness.

GABRIEL FAURÉ

Fauré, whom I greatly admired, was director of the

Conservatoire during my student days; and while still a student, I had the good fortune to find myself in his company on several occasions. Invited one evening to dinner at the home of Madame Sulzbach, a great patron of music (I had frequently played for her on her residence organ), I was indeed surprised to find that Fauré was the *only* other guest!

After dinner my hostess suggested that I improvise at the organ on a theme proposed by Fauré. I admit having the greatest fright of my career. An improvisation in front of Fauré! But I played, and he was most gracious in his praise.

Sometime later another invitation came from Madame Sulzbach. It was the same sort of evening, with the same three people. Fauré said to me, "It appeared to me that you were somewhat nervous the last time you improvised for me. But why? I was on the jury which awarded your first prize in improvisation, and I have followed your progress with interest. Well, let us have another 'go at it' this evening." So I improvised again and I was just as nervous as before.

My last encounter with him took place in Rouen at the Hôtel de France, which at that time had a small concert hall. On this particular evening Fauré accompanied the fine singer Madame Jeanne Raunay in a group of his own songs. He asked me to turn pages for him. As Fauré began the marvelous song "La fleur qui va sur l'eau," he whispered, "You know, it is a very difficult accompaniment, and I am nervous." What humility from this very great man.

PAUL DUKAS

I never had the honor to be a pupil of Paul Dukas, but he always treated me with great kindness. When I published my *Treatise on Improvisation (Traité d'improvisation à l'orgue)*, I was surprised to receive a congratulatory letter from him. This touched me very much.

When Dukas' name was proposed for membership to the Académie, Widor said to me one day, "Go to Paul Dukas' home. I know that he likes and trusts you very much. Tell him for me that he should not hesitate to promote his own cause." Although I felt somewhat uncomfortable about such a mission, I was not able to refuse. Dukas received me cordially, "Well, hello, Dupré, it is very kind of you to come and see me." (I remembered at that moment my first visit with Saint-Saëns.) Feeling a bit ill at ease, I gave him Widor's message.

"You, too?" he asked. "You think that I should promote my nomination to the Académie?"

"That is Widor's advice," I replied, "not mine."

"Ah! I see," Dukas said. "Very well, I shall go to see Widor. He can give me further advice in this matter."

Then he changed the conversation, speaking of his teaching and, above all, of his theories on orchestration. He said something which has remained in my memory. "In orchestrating one should concern himself only with the movement of various voices," seeming to say that picturesque effects should be secondary.

When I started to leave, I excused myself for having disturbed his work. "Please do not worry about it. I compose only for my own pleasure and, therefore, my time is my own."

His death saddened me. I went immediately to see Madame Dukas, and we decided that I would play the organ at the ceremony at the columbarium.

GUSTAVE CHARPENTIER

In May 1940 my father went to Biarritz to stay with my wife's sister Amélie. He died there on the fifth of July of that year. Gustave Charpentier, who had moved away from Paris and who happened to be living at the time across the street from my sister-in-law's home, called there as soon as he had read in the local newspaper of the death of Albert Dupré. He had offered, in view of my unavoidable absence, to be chief mourner — to follow the funeral cortege on foot (he was eighty years old), to participate in the religious service and to attend the burial in the remote cemetery. When trains were running once again, I went to Biarritz to bring my father's body back to Rouen.

It was on my arrival in Biarritz that I learned the touching details of the funeral, and I went to see Gustave Charpentier to express my gratitude. At the conclusion of our visit, as I started to leave, he asked me to return each day at six o'clock during the remainder of my stay in Biarritz. "We shall take a walk together along the sea, and I shall tell you some things which will interest you."

On these walks he spoke of his difficult childhood, of the place his great teacher Massenet occupied in his life, of Debussy, of Paul Dukas — in short, of all the great musicians of his generation. He related his ideas on the theatre, and talked about his famous opera *Louise.* They were captivating moments. When I asked him about his latest composition, he said, just as Dukas had, "I compose for my own pleasure. My time is my own. In fact, for a long time I have not published anything."

FERRUCCIO BUSONI

On each of his trips to Paris, Busoni lunched with Widor at the Restaurant Foyot. One day when I was present — it was in January, 1920 — I heard this astonishing conversation between them. Busoni began,

"Futuristic composers who make such extensive use of chromaticism have forgotten the one thing that would make their music intelligible to other musicians — a chromatic staff!"

"I beg your pardon!" exclaimed Widor.

"That is right. The five lines would represent the five black keys of the keyboard, with a space twice as large between the second and the third lines [to account for the two white notes on the piano]. Such a staff would eliminate all the sharps, flats and naturals in their pieces."

"Would this bizarre notation be accepted?"

"Ever since we have had equal temperament, everyone has accepted the sound of false intervals and the resulting beats. Likewise, one would eventually accept this chromatic staff."

"What would you call the black keys?"

"In German, I would extend the already existing musical alphabet to include I,J,K and L. In French, I would use the syllable names for the white keys, and for the black keys I would keep the consonants but change the vowels: *do* would become *du; ré, ri; fa, fé; sol, sul; la, lé.* (Perhaps it would be wise to replace the French *u* with an *ou,* thereby conforming with Italian usage.)"

"And what about transposition?"

"Which kind? Prepared or at sight?"

"At sight."

"We must forego that. But we would be able to accomplish transposition in the way we print the music. The staves would be printed on regular paper, but the notes would be printed on transparent paper. One could shift the transparent paper up or down the desired number of semitones."

Two years later I "recorded" an improvisation for a player organ at the Skinner Organ Company in America. [This type of organ uses a paper roll similar to that for a player piano.] I was surprised to notice that I could follow easily the perforations during the play-back. Busoni's system came to mind and I explained it to Ernest Skinner, a good musician. "One could use this entire system," he said, "on a perforated roll, and could even indicate, with dotted lines, the measures. I shall experiment with it." He did, but he said to me the following year, "Music without sharps, flats, naturals, different note values, rests, clefs, leger lines and ties — instead only little holes in a roll — that is just a dream!"

FRANCIS PLANTÉ

I made the acquaintance of the illustrious pianist Francis Planté at the Dieppe Casino, where, after a long absence from the concert stage, he was making a brilliant return. I saw him again several times; and while vacationing at Biarritz one summer, I asked him if we might come and see him at Saint-Avit, his residence near Mont-de-Marsan. He invited me and my family to lunch. At eighty-nine years of age he managed to keep a youthful spirit — a gaiety and a miraculous sprightliness. We spent an unforgettable afternoon with him. Very talkative, he related some of his experiences, of which I particularly remember this one. "One day," he said, "I was invited to lunch at the home of Madame

Emile Ollivier (Liszt's daughter Blandine), and I was seated between Liszt and Wagner at the table. I was so excited that I could not swallow my food!"

After lunch he sat at the piano, playing, one after another, preludes and etudes of Chopin and compositions by Albeniz, all with dazzling virtuosity. "Never be afraid," he said as he plunged into a brilliant passage. And his fingers, agile and sure, came to the end without the slightest hesitation.

Together we played some music for two pianos. He was tireless.

Then he said to my daughter, who had played for him, "The years pass quickly. When you are a grandmother, you will be able to tell your grandchildren that you played the piano for a very old man who himself had played at the age of seven for a pupil of Haydn, the Chevalier Neukomme."

We heard Francis Planté for the last time the following year at Orthez in his last concert. He died at the age of ninety-five.

SERGEI RACHMANINOFF

It was through the Russian pianist and composer Nicolas Medtner, with whom we were intimately acquainted, that I met Rachmaninoff. He had been Medtner's childhood companion and fellow-student at the Moscow Conservatory. Both were in the class of Savonoff, the Russian pianist and conductor whom I myself met several times in Widor's home. Rachmaninoff came to Saint-Sulpice one Sunday morning to hear me play, and then he went on with us to Meudon to spend the afternoon.

He told me that upon his arrival in New York, exiled and completely destitute, he went immediately to Steinway and Company, playing the piano to prove his identity. Needless to say, he immediately found the necessary help to start his magnificent career in the United States.

I was struck by his sadness. "Yes," he said to me, "I have had some wonderful opportunities in my life — domestic bliss, triumph, fortune — but I no longer have my Russia. Nostalgia fills my heart."

Fig. 48 – Marcel Dupré at Saint-Sulpice

ALEXANDER GLAZUNOFF

Glazunoff, who had been director of the Saint Petersburg Conservatory, came to live in exile in Boulogne-sur-Seine. When his friend Medtner first brought him to Meudon, he forewarned me that Glazunoff knew of my Bach recitals and would ask me to play several of Bach's works. "But my dear friend," I said to Medtner, "it has been a number of years since I played this series, and I am certainly not able to play just any of these pieces at a moment's notice."

Glazunoff asked to hear about ten of the Cantor's great works, all pieces which were, fortunately, in my current repertoire, and I was able to pass the "test" with honor. I won his admiration.

He had the habit, until he became mortally ill, of coming almost every Sunday to Saint-Sulpice. Seated beside me on the organ bench, he listened to me improvise. He came as frequently to Meudon. His knowledge of music was prodigious, and his conversation, charming. He had a deep admiration for Liszt and he related the following story to me:

I was twenty years old and I had just finished orchestrating my first symphony. Knowing that Liszt was very interested in young musicians and having saved some money, I wrote to him something like this: "Maître, if you would be willing to look at the score of my symphony, I shall come to Weimar to show it to you. I want to know whether you think I should continue to compose or whether I should give it up." Liszt replied immediately, inviting me to come to see him. My heart was thumping! I went to Weimar. Liszt welcomed me with these words, "You are courageous, young man." Then with great care he played through my symphony on the piano, from the first note to the last. I was in agony awaiting his verdict. Then I heard him say, and for a moment I thought I was dreaming, "I have made a decision. I shall include it this year on one of my concerts." "But maître," I replied, "I must have explained myself badly. I would never have dreamed of asking you. . .I only wanted to have your opinion. . ." "I know," Liszt broke in jovially. "I shall even pay for your travel and lodging expenses so that you can come and hear the rehearsals. Let me have your score. I shall take the responsibility of having the orchestral parts copied.'' Liszt kept his word, and he himself conducted the performance.

In recalling this wonderful event in his life, Glazunoff was visibly moved. One can understand the devotion he had for Liszt, whose goodness and generosity are legendary.

Fig. 49 – Dupré plays for Mass at Saint-Sulpice

EPILOGUE

Now I shall close. My life since my retirement from the Conservatoire has taken on a slower pace, and I have limited little by little the number of my concert engagements.

I decided that the recitals that I gave in October of 1970 in Troyes and in Tours would be the last. They were the 2,177th and 2,178th of my career, a career in which the organ, my chosen instrument, frequently caused me problems. A piano may be more or less beautiful, but it is always basically the same instrument. A violinist takes his instrument with him, like a friend. But the concert organist many times finds himself at an unfamiliar instrument on which the number of stops, their arrangement on the console, and other particular features are completely new to him. He must assimilate all these things in a minimum amount of time. He can also be the victim, in the middle of a piece, of a cipher (a spontaneous and continuous sounding of a note), an abrupt intrusion in the music. I have a painful memory of such an accident during one of my first concerts in London. I was playing my own Prelude and Fugue in G minor when, at the beginning of the fugue, a loud cipher started. What was I to do? Stop playing? In a flash I changed keys and transposed the entire fugue. Only those persons who knew the piece were aware of what had happened, but I had had some very difficult moments.

Worse things have happened to me. The following story, which I have often laughed about, but which was far from humorous at the time, took place in Wales.

I was welcomed cordially at the train station by the organist of the church where I was to play that evening. I asked, as usual, when I might practice on the organ.

"Oh, that would be useless. That would not serve any purpose. I have a capricious instrument. You pull this stop, and you get that one. If you pull a viola stop, you get a trumpet, and so forth. You would waste time in preparing registrations for your pieces. So I am planning to take you on a nice tour of the countryside."

"But under these conditions, I am not going to be able to give my concert. Why have you engaged me?"

"I wished to meet you and to hear you play."

"But what is the audience going to think?"

"They have been listening to the organ in this sorry state for years. You have nothing to worry about."

Disarmed, I insisted, nevertheless, on going to meet the "rebel." Alas, my colleague had not exaggerated, and I was obliged to do "juggling acts" in this concert. Fortunately the reactions of the public were such that I breathed a bit easier. But what an evening!

Happily, the counterpart exists — the joy of playing a magnificent organ!

In spite of my decision to stop performing in public, I shall make one exception. The BBC has invited me to participate as an "honored guest" in a festival program which will take place in London on the sixteenth of April of this year [1971]. It will be in Royal Albert Hall, in honor of its one hundredth anniversary. I have accepted.

I confess that this invitation touched me deeply, especially since I had discontinued my concerts in Great Britain several years ago. So, in the same hall where I made my international debut a half a century ago, I shall end my concert career.

Meanwhile, my quiet life in our very dear home in Meudon, that home which has sheltered us and the wonderful organ of my dear maître Alexandre Guilmant for forty-six years, is filled with much happiness. The weeks pass, each one crowned with the joy of finding myself on Sunday mornings, as I have since the age of twenty, before the five manuals of Saint-Sulpice's royal instrument, surrounded by the many dear friends who continue to gather there.

****

If life has brought me many trials and tribulations, it has also brought me many rich blessings. I would not be able to lay down my pen without speaking of the adored companion of my long life to whom I owe so very much. Agrégée de l'Université,* she terminated her short teaching career at the Lycée Victor Duruy in Paris in order to consecrate herself to my career. "Consecrate" is the word! As secretary and collaborator she freed me from cares and many burdensome tasks. She knew, with tenderness and devotion, how to create a favorable atmosphere for my work in our pleasant and peaceful home, a home enhanced by the presence of our dear grandchildren.

Meudon, 19 February 1971

Madame Dupré is an Agrégée in English. Difficult to obtain, this certification is awarded through competition and not through examination. It permits one to teach on both secondary and college levels.

Fig. 50 — Marcel Dupré leaves Saint-Sulpice

APPENDICES

Appendix A

CALENDAR OF DUPRÉ'S LIFE

1886 - Marcel Dupré born in Rouen (May 3) at 16, rue du Vert-Buisson. Son of Albert Dupré, organist and leading Rouen musician, and the former Marie-Alice Chauvière, cellist. Baptized Marcel Jean Jules (June 17) in Saint-Ouen, Rouen: M. Jules Lesueur, a friend of the family, and Mme. Jeanne-Hébert Visinet, a great-aunt, are the godparents.

1888 - Dupré family moves to 12, rue du Vert-Buisson.

1891 - Developed osteomyelitis in the right collar bone; surgery to remove the diseased portion of bone.

1893 - Begins piano lessons with his father; later the same year he begins organ lessons with his father.

1894 - First performance in public: opens the inaugural recital on the organ in the Church of the Immaculate Conception, Elbeuf, playing Bach's Prelude and Fugue in E minor.

1895 - Begins harmony and counterpoint lessons with his father.

1896 - Plays several organ solos at the Rouen Exposition: Bach's Fugue in G minor ("Little") and a piece by Guilmant. Albert Dupré has a small organ built for his home.

1897 - Receives first Communion in the chapel of the Lycée Corneille, Rouen.

1898 - Begins organ lessons with Guilmant. He is appointed organist of Saint-Vivien, Rouen; participates, with Guilmant, in the inaugural recital on the new organ (June 23), playing Bach's Prelude and Fugue in C minor.

1901 - On his fifteenth birthday, Dupré's first cantata *Jacob's Dream (Le Songe de Jacob)* is performed by L'Accord Parfait under his father's direction.

1902 - Dupré is admitted to the Paris Conservatoire: receiving a first prize in piano, class of Diémer (1905); a first prize (unanimous) in organ and improvisation, class of Guilmant (1907); a first prize in fugue, class of Widor (1909).

1906 - Appointed assistant organist to Widor at Saint-Sulpice, Paris.

1912 - Composes first notable organ work: *Three Preludes and Fugues,* op. 7. (First Performance: Paris, Salle Gaveau, 1917, by Dupré)

1914 - Dupré is awarded the Grand Prix de Rome (July 4) for his cantata *Psyché.* (First Performance: Rouen, Théâtre des Arts, 1919). Begins work in a hospital pharmacy, having been disqualified for military service because of the operation on his right collar bone. Continues this war effort until 1916.

1916 - Dupré substitutes for Louis Vierne at Notre-Dame Cathedral while the latter is receiving treatment for his eyes in Switzerland. What was to have been a five-month substitution lasted until 1921.

1917 - Composes *De Profundis,* a choral work written in memory of World War I dead. (First Performance: Paris, Église des Blancs-Manteaux, 1924, the Lamoureux Orchestra under the direction of Paul Paray)

1919 - Opens an organ studio in Paris, rue Leverrier. Composes *Fifteen Pieces* (Vêpres du Commun), op. 18, for organ. (First Performance: London, Royal Albert Hall, 1920)

1920 - Dupré performs from memory the complete organ works of J. S. Bach in a series of ten recitals during January, February and March, at the Paris Conservatoire. Widor, speaking at the last program, said publically, "We must all regret, my dear Dupré, the absence from our midst of the person whose name is foremost in our thoughts today — the great Johann Sebastian Bach. Rest assured that if he had been here, he would have embraced you and pressed you to his heart." London debut at Royal Albert Hall (December 9): the Prince of Wales, the future Edward VIII, is present. In the following years, Dupré concertizes in England, Scotland, Ireland, Belgium, Holland, Germany, Austria, Switzerland, Italy, Spain and Portugal.

1921 -   He performs again the complete organ works of Bach from memory, this time at the Trocadéro (replaced by the Palais de Chaillot). Makes his American debut (November 17) on the organ in the John Wanamaker Store in New York City, closing the program with an improvised four-movement organ symphony: the press calls the feat "A musical miracle." In all he plays eighteen recitals in New York and Philadelphia to inaugurate the Wanamaker organs: his programs are devoted to works of Bach and French composers.

1922 -   Completes a second American tour, playing ninety-four concerts from coast to coast. Composes *Cortège et Litanie*, one of five pieces of incidental music for a dramatic production, giving it its final form as one of four piano pieces. Subsequently he transcribes it for organ solo, then for organ and orchestra. (First Performance: New York, John Wanamaker Store, 1923)

1923 -   Composes *Suite Bretonne* for organ. (First Performance: New York, 1923) Named Chevalier de la Légion d'honneur. Makes a third American tour, playing 110 concerts. Moves into an apartment in the rue Delambre in Paris. Composes *Variations sur un Noël* for organ. (First Performance: United States, 1923)

1924 -   Completes his first organ symphony, *Symphonie-Passion*, a four-movement work first conceived as an improvisation (December 8, 1921). (First Performance: London, Westminster Cathedral, 1924) Marries (April 23) the former Jeanne Pascouau in Saint-Sulpice; Widor is a witness. Makes his fourth American tour. Publishes *Gammes de pédale pour orgue (Pedal Scales for Organ).*

1925 -   Purchases a home in the Parisian suburb of Meudon, adding a small auditorium to house a residence organ (acquired from the estate of Alexandre Guilmant) and to provide teaching accomodations for his growing number of pupils from France and abroad. Converts a small building on the grounds into a museum where are kept the original Cavaillé-Coll console to Guilmant's organ, as well as manuscripts, photographs of the organs he has played, etc. Publishes his *Traité d'improvisation à l'orgue (Treatise on Improvisation at the Organ).*

1926 -   Appointed professor of organ at the Paris Conservatoire, succeeding Gigout: remains in this post for twenty-eight years, training such organists as Fleury, Messiaen, Langlais, Grunenwald, Jehan Alain, Marie-Claire Alain, Demessieux, Falcinelli, Cochereau, Marie-Madeleine Duruflé, Joulain and Guillou.

1927 - Publishes his *Méthode d'Orgue (Method for the Organ)*. Appointed professor of organ at both L'École normale de Musique and at the American Conservatory at Fontainebleau.

1928 - Completes his Symphony in G minor for organ and orchestra.

1929 - Makes his fifth American tour.

1930 - Elected a member of the Académie de Rouen. Composes his Second Organ Symphony.

1931 - Composes *Le Chemin de la Croix (The Stations of the Cross)* (inspired by the poem of Paul Claudel), following its conception as an improvisation in Brussels. (First Performance: Paris, Trocadéro, 1932)

1933 - Completes a sixth American tour. Death of his mother, Mme. Albert Dupré (August 7).

1934 - Dupré succeeds Charles-Marie Widor as organist of Saint-Sulpice. Composes his Concerto in E minor for organ and orchestra. (First Performance: Holland, 1938) Between 1934 and 1936 he publishes six textbooks on various subjects: harmony, counterpoint, fugue, plainchant accompaniment, beginning exercises in improvisation, and a study in acoustics.

1935 - Receives the rank of Officier de la Légion d'honneur. Composes *Poème Héroïque* for organ, brass and snare drum. (First Performance: reopening of the severely damaged Cathedral of Verdun, 1937)

1937 - Plays for the wedding of the Duke of Windsor and Wallis Simpson in the Château de Candé. Makes his seventh American tour. Awarded a Doctor of Music degree *(honoris causa)* by Baldwin-Wallace Conservatory.

1938 - Begins publication of his editions of the organ works of J. S. Bach; publishes subsequently editions of organ music of other masters: various pre-Bach composers, Handel, Liszt, Mendelssohn, Schumann and Franck.

1939 - Plays a recital on the "Magic Key Hour," broadcast from Meudon to America via short-wave radio. World tour (eighth in the United States), playing sixty concerts in the United States, several of which were in the Temple of Religion at the New York World's Fair, and twenty-five concerts in Australia. Arrives home as World War II erupts.

1940 - Death of his father, Albert Dupré (July 5). Spends the war years (1940-1945) in Meudon, where he continues to compose and to prepare his editions of the great masters; the windows in his *salle d'orgue* are shattered by a bomb, but the organ escapes damage.

1941 - Composes *Évocation,* dedicated to the memory of Albert Dupré. (First Performance: Rouen, Saint-Ouen, 1942)

1946 - Appointed the director of the American Conservatory at Fontainebleau. Completes his ninth American tour, including a series of master classes and recitals at the University of Chicago.

1948 - Awarded the rank of Commandeur de la Légion d'honneur. Makes his tenth and final transcontinental American tour.

1953 - Receives a doctor's degree *(honoris causa)* from the Pontifical Gregorian Institute in Rome. Accorded a private audience with Pope Pius XII (November 23).

1954 - Named the director of the Paris Conservatoire continuing in this position until 1956.

1956 - Composes *La France au Calvaire,* dedicated to the memory of his parents. (First Performance: Rouen, The Cathedral, June 25, 1956, Dupré conducting) Elected to the Institut de France, member of the Académie des Beaux-Arts.

1957 - Decorated with Commandeur de l'Ordre des Arts et des Lettres.

1958 - Visits America, playing recitals in Detroit's Ford Auditorium and in New York's St. Thomas Church, where he makes a series of recordings.

1959 - Composes *Nymphéas* for organ — a suite of eight pieces inspired by the collection of Monet's paintings on permanent display in the Orangerie gallery of the Louvre. The work must be played on the organ in the composer's home, for certain mechanical devices found only on this organ are employed. (A recording of this work made in 1973 by Rolande Falcinelli is played three times a week in the Orangerie.)

1962 - Plays a recital at Saint-Sulpice (May 3) for the one-hundredth anniversary of the organ. Visits America for the last time, playing a recital in Detroit.

1966 - Concert at Saint-Sulpice (May 8) by former pupils of Dupré in honor of his eightieth birthday. Decorated with Knight Commander of the Order of St. Gregory. Awarded l'Ordre national du Mérite.

1970 - Organization (July 10) of L'Association des Amis de l'Art de Marcel Dupré. Plays his 2177th and 2178th recitals at Troyes and Tours.

1971 - Completes a book of personal recollections, published in 1972 by Éditions Bornemann. Dupré makes his last concert appearance (April 16) in Royal Albert Hall, London. Performance of his *De Profundis* in Saint-Sulpice (May 7) in honor of his eighty-fifth birthday; he receives homage from many distinguished pupils. Organ recital (May 13) by Rolande Falcinelli at Saint-Sulpice in honor of his birthday: Dupré closes the program with an improvisation.

May 30 — Death of Marcel Dupré at his home in Meudon. Had played two masses (Feast of the Pentecost) that morning at Saint-Sulpice. Funeral (June 3) at Saint-Sulpice: eulogized by academicians Jacques Carlu and Emmanuel Bondeville; the great nave is filled with clergy, government representatives, family, former pupils, and friends. Burial in Meudon.

Appendix B

CATALOGUE OF DUPRÉ'S WORKS

(Based on the composer's classification as found in his personal notebook)

Youthful Works
(Unpublished except as noted)

1895 - *Prière* in G, organ
       Fugue in C (three voices), organ
1897 - *La Fleur*, voice
1898 - *Oudlette dans le Puits*, voice (published)
       Minuet, for piano, violin and cello (later orchestrated for strings)
       Marche des Paysans, piano (later orchestrated for strings)
1899 - Barcarolle, piano
       Canon (two voices), piano
       Danse du Tambourin, piano
1900 - Waltz in C-sharp minor, piano
       Fugue in F (two voices)
1901 - Fugue in A minor (four voices), organ
       Sonata (Allegro) in C, trio
       Le Songe de Jacob, cantata
1902 - *Pièce caractéristique*, piano

Student Compositions
(Unpublished)

1905 - *Le Récif de Corail*, voice (poem by Heredia)
1907 - *Lointain*, voice
       Le Colibri, voice
       Romance sans Paroles, piano
       String Quartet (Allegro)
1908 - Double Quartet
1909 - *Ton Souvenir*, voice (poem by Samain)
1910 - Impromptu in B minor, piano
       Fugue in G, piano
       Hantise, voice (later orchestrated)
       Two Cadenzas for Beethoven's Concerto in C

1912 - *Sur les Flots,* voice (poem by Hugo)
      Pourquoi, voice (poem by Hugo)
      Consolation, voice

Chorus
(Unpublished)

1912 - *Cortège antique*
      Crépuscule
      Tempête
      Aurore
      Danse orientale
1913 - *Cantique de Racine*
      Soir sur la Plaine
1914 - *Juin*

Cantatas
(Unpublished)

1911 - *Acis et Galatée*
1912 - *Yanitze*
1913 - *Ismaïl*
      Faust et Hélène
1914 - *Selma*

Works Without Opus Numbers
(Unpublished except as noted)

1915 - *La Tentation de Saint-Antoine* (incidental music)
      Agnus Dei, baritone and organ
1924 - *Noël de France,* voice and piano (published by Leduc)
1944 - *Résonances,* symphonic etude for instrumental soloists and organ
1948 - *Épithalame,* organ (for Marguerite)

Works with Opus Numbers

Opus	Date of Composition	Title	Publisher
1	1911 -	*Les Normands,* chorus and orchestra	
2	1913 -	*Élévation,* harmonium	Abbé Joubert

3	1915 -	*Le Glaive*, soprano and orchestra (poem by Hugo)	-
4	1914 -	*Psyché*, cantata	Leduc
5	1909 -	Sonata, violin and piano	Leduc
		Allegro - Andante - Rondo	
6	1914 -	Four Songs (orchestrated)	Leduc
		Roses dans la Nuit (poem by Louÿs)	
		Sous la Pluie (poem by Louÿs)	
		Marquise (poem by Sylvestre)	
		Les deux Sœurs (poem by Hugo)	
7	1912 -	Three Preludes and Fugues, organ	Leduc
		B major - F minor - G minor	
8	1912 -	Fantasy, piano and orchestra	Leduc
9	1916 -	Four Motets, four voices and two organs	Leduc
		O Salutaris	
		Ave Maria	
		Tantum ergo	
		Laudate	
10	1917 -	Two Pieces, clarinet and piano	Leroy
11	1910 -	*A l'Amie perdue*, voice (orchestrated)	Leduc
		Nos Yeux seuls	
		Quand je l'embrasserai	
		Si mon Amour	
		Ah, les divins Moments	
		Je ne t'ai pas connue	
		Viens chercher sur mon Cœur	
		Une Lueur au Ciel	
12	1916 -	Six Preludes, piano	Leduc
13	1916 -	Three Pieces, violoncello	Leduc
14	1915 -	*Marche militaire*, piano	-
15	1912 -	*Orientale* (orchestrated)	-
16	1919 -	Scherzo in F minor, organ	Leduc
17	1917 -	*De Profundis*, cantata for soloists, chorus, orchestra and organ	Leduc
18	1920 -	Fifteen Pieces *(Vêpres du commun)*, organ	Gray*
		Five Antiphons on Psalms	
		Four Versets on *Ave maris stella*	
		Six Versets on *Magnificat*	
19	1922 -	Four Pieces, piano	Leduc
		Étude	
		Chanson	
		Air de Ballet	
		Cortège et Litanie (arranged by the composer for organ solo and for organ and orchestra)	(Leduc)

Indicates a publication of The H. W. Gray Co., Inc., now H. W. Gray Publications, a Division of Belwin-Mills Publishing Corp.

20	1923 -	*Variations sur un Noël,* organ	Leduc
21	1923 -	*Suite Bretonne,* organ	Leduc
		Berceuse	
		Fileuse	
		Les Cloches de Perros-Guirec	
22	1924 -	Variations in C-sharp minor, piano	Leduc
23	1924 -	*Symphonie-Passion,* organ	Leduc
		Le Monde dans l'attente du Sauveur	
		Nativité	
		Crucifixion	
		Résurrection	
24	1926 -	*Lamento,* organ	Leduc
25	1927 -	Symphony in G minor, organ and orchestra	Salabert
26	1930 -	Second Symphony, organ	Salabert
		Prelude - Intermezzo - Toccata	
27	1931 -	Seven Pieces, organ	Bornemann*
		Souvenir	
		Marche	
		Pastorale	
		Carillon	
		Canon	
		Légende	
		Final	
28	1931 -	Seventy-nine Chorales, organ	Gray
		(Preparatory study for Bach's chorale-preludes,	
		employing chorales used by Bach)	
29	1931 -	*Le Chemin de la Croix,* organ	Durand
30	1932 -	Ballade, piano and organ	Gray
31	1934 -	Concerto in E minor, organ and orchestra	Bornemann
32	1935 -	*Trois Élévations,* organ	Herelle
33	1935 -	*Poème Héroïque,* for organ, brass, and snare drum	Gray
		(arranged by the composer for organ solo)	(Gray)
34	1936 -	A. *Angélus,* organ	Herelle
		B. *Ave verum Corpus,* mixed voices and string orchestra	-
35	1938 -	Variations on Two Themes, piano and organ	Gray
36	1939 -	Three Preludes and Fugues, organ	Gray
		E minor - A major - C major	
37	1941 -	*Évocation,* symphonic poem for organ	Bornemann
38	1942 -	Sixteen Chorales *(Le Tombeau de Titelouze),* organ	Gray
		(Based on sixteen liturgical hymns)	

*Indicates a publication of Éditions Bornemann, Paris,· available in the United States from Belwin-Mills Publishing Corp.

| 39 | 1943 - | Suite in F minor, organ | Bornemann |

Allegro agitato - Cantabile - Scherzando - Finale

| 40 | 1944 - | Offrande à la Vierge, organ | Bornemann |

       Virgo Mater

       Mater dolorosa

       Virgo Mediatrix

| 41 | 1945 - | A. *Deux Esquisses,* organ | Bornemann |

       E minor - B-flat minor

| | | B. *Esquisse* (discovered 1975), organ | Bornemann |

       C major

42	1946 -	Sinfonia, piano and organ	Gray
43	1946 -	Paraphrase on the *Te Deum,* organ	Gray
44	1947 -	*Vision,* symphonic poem for organ	Bornemann
45	1948 -	Eight Short Preludes, keyboard	McLaughlin & Reilly

       Salve Regina

       Virgo Dei Genitrix

       Pange lingua

       Sacris solemnis

       Alma Redemptoris Mater

       Ave verum Corpus

       Lauda Sion

       Verbum supernum

46	1948 -	*Miserere mei,* organ	Bornemann
47	1949 -	Psalm XVIII *(Coeli enarrant gloriam Dei),* symphonic poem for organ	Bornemann
48	1952 -	*Six Antiennes pour le Temps de Noël,* organ	Bornemann

       Ecce Dominus veniet

       Omnipotens sermo tuus

       Tecum principium

       Germinavit radix Jesse

       Stella ista

       Lumen ad revelationem

| 49 | 1956 - | *La France au Calvaire,* oratorio for soloists, chorus, orchestra and organ | Bornemann |

       Prologue

       Saint-Denis

       Sainte-Clotilde

       Saint-Louis

       Jeanne d'Arc

       Saint-Vincent de Paul

       Sainte-Thérèse de Lisieux

       Gloria du Christ

| 50 | 1956 - | Twenty-four Inventions, organ | Bornemann |
| 51 | 1957 - | *Triptyque,* organ | Bornemann |

       Chaconne - Musette - Dithyrambe

| 52 | 1958 - | Quartet in D minor for violin, viola, violoncello and organ | Gray |

       Prelude - Scherzando - Larghetto - Rondo

53	1958 -	Two Motets	Coecilia
		Memorare, O piissima Virgo Maria, soprano	
		Alma Redemptoris, mixed voices	
54	1959 -	*Nymphéas*, organ	
		Rayons	
		Brumes	
		Les Fleurs	
		Temps lourd	
		Brises	
		Nocturne	
		Aube	
		Vapeurs dorées	
55	1960 -	Trio in F minor for violin, violoncello and organ	Gray
		Allegro - Adagio - Finale	
56	1960 -	*Annonciation*, two meditations for organ	Bornemann
57	1962 -	Chorale and Fugue (Easter Alleluia), organ	Bornemann
58	1963 -	Three Hymns, organ	Bornemann
		Matins - Vespers - Lauds	
59	1963 -	Two Chorales, organ	Galleon
60	1964 -	Sonata in A minor, violoncello and organ	Gray
61	1965 -	*In Memoriam*, organ	Bornemann
		Prelude - Allegretto - Meditation	
		Quodlibet - Ricercar - Postlude	
62	1967 -	*Entrée, Canzona, Sortie*, organ	Eulenburg
		(In "Contemporary Music for Liturgical Use" Vol. IV)	
63	1968 -	Four Modal Fugues, organ	Bornemann
		Dorian - Phrygian - Locrian - Ionian	
64	1969 -	*Deux Antiennes*, organ	Bornemann
		Regina coeli by Marcel Dupré	
		Salve Regina by Rolande Falcinelli	
65	1969 -	*Vitrail*, organ	Bornemann

Textbooks

Date	Translated Title	Publisher
1914 -	Manual on Harmony	-
1924 -	Pedal Scales for Organ	Leduc
1925 -	Treatise on Improvisation	Leduc
1927 -	Method for the Organ	Leduc
1927 -	Organ Building	-
1934 -	Treatise on Harmony (I and II)	Leduc
1935 -	Counterpoint	Leduc
1935 -	Beginning Course in Harmony	-
1936 -	Fugue	Leduc
1936 -	Plainsong Accompaniment	Leduc
1936 -	Manual on Acoustics	Herelle
1936 -	Preparatory Exercises for Free Improvisation	Leduc
1937 -	Beginning Course in Orchestration	-
1937 -	Composition	-
1946 -	Philosophy of Music	-

Appendix C

CATALOGUE OF DUPRÉ'S EDITIONS AND TRANSCRIPTIONS

Critical Editions of Standard Organ Works
(Published by Éditions Bornemann)

Bach	Complete Organ Works (twelve volumes)
Handel	Sixteen Concertos (three volumes)
Liszt	Three Works (one volume)
Old Masters	Thirty-six Pieces (published separately)
Mendelssohn	Three Preludes and Fugues, Six Sonatas (one volume)
Schumann	Six Etudes (Canons), Four Sketches, Six Fugues on B.A.C.H. (one volume)
Franck	Six Pieces, Three Pieces, Three Chorales (four volumes)

(Published by Belaieff)

Glazunoff	Two Preludes and Fugues, Fantaisie

Transcriptions

(Based on the composer's listing in his personal notebook; unpublished except as noted)

For Orchestra

1924 -	Bach	Toccata, Adagio and Fugue in C (organ)
1925 -	Liszt	*Saint François de Paul marchant sur les Flots* (piano)
1927 -	Vivaldi-Bach	Concerto in A minor (organ)
1930 -	Liszt	Fantasia and Fugue on *Ad nos, ad salutarum undam* (organ)
1948 -	Liszt	Variations on *Weinen, Klagen, Sorgen, Zagen* (organ)

For Piano and Organ

Undated -	Dupré	Symphony in G minor, op. 25 (organ and orchestra) (published by Salabert)
1945 -	Balakireff	*Islamey:* Oriental Fantasy (piano)
1946 -	Franck	Symphonic Variations (piano and orchestra)
Undated -	Dupré	Concerto in E minor, op. 31 (organ and orchestra) (published by Bornemann)

For Organ

1912 -	Franck	"Symphonic Interlude" from the oratorio *Redemption* (published by Bornemann)
1935 -	Mozart	Fugue in C minor (two pianos) (published by Leduc)
1937 -	Mendelssohn	"Scherzo" from incidental music to *A Midsummer Night's Dream* (orchestra)
1944 -	Borodin	*In the Steppes of Central Asia* (orchestra)
1945 -	Dukas	*L'Apprenti Sorcier* (orchestra)
Undated -	Schubert*	*L'Abeille* (violin)
Undated -	Fauré	"In paradisum" from *Requiem* (in preparation: Belwin-Mills)
Undated -	Fauré	"Nocturne" from incidental music to *Shylock*
Undated -	Schumann	*L'Oiseau prophète* (piano)
Undated -	Chopin	Etude in F minor (piano)
Undated -	Mendelssohn	Prelude No. 6 in B-flat (piano)

*Of Dresden

Appendix D

RECONSTRUCTIONS AND RECORDINGS OF IMPROVISATIONS BY DUPRÉ

Reconstructions*

Variations on "Adeste fidelis," from Skinner Organ Company Pipe Organ Roll No. 762 by Rollin Smith, published by Belwin-Mills Publishing Corp.

Zephyrs (An improvisation for organ on a theme by Leopold Stokowski), from Aeolian Duo-Art Pipe Organ Roll No. 3359 by Rollin Smith, published by Belwin-Mills Publishing Corp.

Recordings

Double Fugue
October 12, 1969
Organ: Notre-Dame Cathedral, Paris
AAAMD** 713.067

Eleven Versets
December 8, 1957
Organ: Saint-Louis des Invalides, Paris
Erato LDE 3082

Four Improvisations
July 20, 1969
Organ: not identified
Advent 5011

Music for the Mass
a) December 13, 1970
Organ: Saint-Sulpice, Paris
AAAMD** 713.021
b) January 17 and 24, 1971
Organ: Saint-Sulpice, Paris
AAAMD** 713.046

*Although it is known that Dupré made numerous organ rolls, these are the only reconstructions that are published.

**L'Association des Amis de l'Art de Marcel Dupré, 21 Boulevard Exelmans, 75016, Paris.

c)   January 24 and 31, 1971
       Organ: Saint-Sulpice, Paris
       AAAMD** 713.061
d)   February 7 and 14, 1971
       Organ: Saint-Sulpice, Paris
       AAAMD** M743.024
e)   March 21, 1971
       Organ: Saint-Sulpice, Paris
       AAAMD** 753.005

On a theme of Samuel Ducommun
       November 30, 1952
       Organ: Collégiale de Neufchâtel
       AAAMD** MS 733.030

Symphony in four movements
       October 12, 1969
       Organ: Notre-Dame Cathedral, Paris
       AAAMD** 713.067

Voluntary on a theme of Rolande Falcinelli
       May 13, 1971
       Organ: Saint-Sulpice, Paris
       AAAMD** 713.054

**L'Association des Amis de l'Art de Marcel Dupré, 21 Boulevard Exelmans, 75016, Paris.

Appendix E

RECORDINGS BY DUPRÉ*

This appendix, compiled from information supplied by M. Pierre Lafond, lists commercial phonograph recordings of organ music made by Marcel Dupré from 1926 until 1971. Every endeavor has been made to establish an accurate and complete listing; and any errors and any omissions of original "releases," "re-issues," or "re-pressings" by affiliates are regretted. Some recordings are still available in monaural and/or stereophonic sound. Unless otherwise indicated, all recordings are on twelve-inch records playing at 33 1/3 r.p.m. Complete information about a record is given only once, and reference to this original listing is made to its number in this appendix; e.g., "See No. 5" indicates that a particular composition is on the recording completely listed under entry No. 5.

Works of Dupré

1   *Berceuse,* from *Suite Bretonne*
                    Organ: Queen's Hall, London
                    His Master's Voice D 1722, 78 r.p.m.

2   *Carillon,* from Seven Pieces
                    Dupré at Saint-Sulpice, Vol. II
                    Olympian Series
                    Mercury MG 50229, SR 90229

3   *Chemin de la Croix, Le*
                    Collector's Series
                    Organ: Saint-Sulpice, Paris
                    Westminster W9349

4   Chorale and Fugue
            a)   Dupré interprète ses propres Œuvres
                    Trésors Classiques
                    Organ: Saint-Ouen, Rouen
                    Philips 835.763 LY
            b)   Extraordinaire Marcel Dupré, L'
                    Organs: Saint-Sulpice, Paris and
                        Saint-Ouen, Rouen
                    Philips 658.010

*See also Appendix D.

5-11   Chorales, from Seventy-nine Chorales
       (5) *By the rivers of Babylon*
               Organ: Dupré residence, Meudon
               Lumen 3.26.013
       (6) *Deck thyself, O beloved soul*
               See No. 5
       (7) *How bright shineth the day-star*
               See No. 5
       (8) *In quiet joy*
          a)   See No. 4a
          b)   See No. 4b
          c)   See No. 5
       (9) *Our Father in heaven*
               See No. 5
       (10) *Out of the depth have I cried unto Thee*
               See No. 5
       (11) *This day full of gladness*
               See No. 5

12   *Cortège et Litanie*
               See No. 2

13   *Final*, from Seven Pieces
               See No. 2

14   Hymn: *Iste Confessor*, from Sixteen Chorales
          a)   See No. 4a
          b)   See No. 4b

15   *Lamento*
               See No. 2

16-19   Preludes and Fugues
       (16) C major
          a)   Dupré à Saint-Sulpice, Vol. V
               Mercury MG 50231, SR 90231
               Philips 120.576 MLL
          b)   See No. 4b
       (17) E minor
          a)   See No. 4b
          b)   See No. 16a
       (18) G minor
          a)   His Master's Voice 454, 10 in., 78 r.p.m.
          b)   Disque Gramophone P715,10 in., 78 r.p.m.
          c)   Olympian Series
               Organ: St. Thomas, New York
               Mercury MG 50169, SR 90169

(19) A-flat major
    a)   See No. 4b
    b)   See No. 16a

20   *Symphonie-Passion*
        See No. 4a

21   Toccata on *Ave maris stella*, from Fifteen Pieces
    a)   See No. 4a
    b)   See No. 4b

22   *Triptyque*
        See No. 18c

23   *Variations sur un Noël*
        See No. 2

Works of Bach

24   Aria, from Suite in D (arr. Dupré)
        Organ: Queen's Hall, London
        His Master's Voice D1588, 78 r.p.m.
        Victor 7119, 78 r.p.m.

25-41   Chorale Preludes (English titles from Dupré's edition of the complete organ works of J. S. Bach, published by Éditions Bornemann, Paris)
(25) *Abide with us, O Lord*, BWV 649
        Dupré à Saint-Sulpice, Vol. IV
        Olympian Series
        Mercury MG 50230, SR 90230
(26) *Awake, the watchmen cry out*, BWV 645
    a)   Organ: Queen's Hall, London
        His Master's Voice E471, 10 in., 78 r.p.m.
    b)   See No. 25
    c)   World Series
        Organ: Saint-Ouen, Rouen
        Philips PHC 9017
    d)   Trésors Classiques
        Philips M 641.764, S 835.764
(27) *Before Thy throne I now appear*, BWV 668
        See No. 26c
(28) *Christ our Lord to Jordan came*, BWV 684
    a)   See No. 26a
    b)   See No. 26c

(29) *Come now, Saviour of the heathen*, BWV 659
                Organ: Saint-Sulpice, Paris
                Lumen LD 3.106
                Overtone OV 13

(30) *Comest Thou, Jesus, down from heaven to earth?*, BWV 650
                See No 25

(31) *From heaven a host of angels came*, BWV 650
                See No. 26c

(32) *Glory to God on high*, BWV 662
                See No. 26c

(33) *He that suffereth God to guide him*, BWV 647
                See No. 25

(34) *I bid thee farewell*, BWV 735 (or BWV 736)
                His Master's Voice DA 4000, 10 in., 78 r.p.m.

(35) *In Thee is Joy*, BWV 615
    a)   Organ: Alexandra Palace, London
            His Master's Voice D1873, 78 r.p.m.
            Victor 7421, 78 r.p.m.
            Victor 11-0017, 78 r.p.m.
    b)   See No. 26c

(36) *Kyrie, God, Holy Spirit*, BWV 671
                See No. 26c

(37) *My soul doth magnify the Lord*, BWV 648
                See No. 25

(38) *O man, bemoan thy grievous sins*, BWV 622
    a)   Organ: Saint-Sulpice, Paris
            Lumen LD 2.133, 10 in.
    b)   See No. 26c
    c)   See No. 29

(39) *Through Adam's fall*, BWV 637
                See No. 26c

(40) *We all believe in one God*, BWV 680
    a)   See No. 38a
    b)   See No. 26c
    c)   See No. 29

(41) *Whither shall I flee?*, BWV 646
                See No. 25

42-43   Fantasias
(42) C minor
                See No. 25
(43) G major
                See No. 25

44-45 Fantasias and Fugues
    (44) C minor
                Organ: Queen's Hall, London
                His Master's Voice, D1356, 78 r.p.m.
                Disque Gramophone, W952, 78 r.p.m.
                Victor 9284, 78 r.p.m.
                Victor 11-0018, 78 r.p.m.
    (45) G minor, BWV 542
                Decca LM 4513, 10 in.
                London LS-137

46 Fugue in G minor
                Lumen 3.26.011, 78 r.p.m.

47 Passacaglia and Fugue in C minor, BWV 582
        a)   Organ: Queen's Hall, London
                His Master's Voice D1765/66, 78 r p.m.
        b)   See No. 29

48-53 Preludes and Fugues
    (48) C minor
                Organ: Alexandra Palace, London
                His Master's Voice GD 2003, 78 r.p.m.
    (49) D major, BWV 532
                Dupré à Saint-Sulpice, Vol. I
                Olympian Series
                Mercury MG 50227, SR 90227
    (50) E-flat major, BWV 552
                See No. 38a
    (51) E minor ("Wedge"), BWV 548
        a)   Organ: Queen's Hall, London
                His Master's Voice DB 4000/1, 78 r.p.m.
        b)   See No. 49
        c)   Organ: Collégiale de Neufchâtel
                AAAMD* MS 733.030
    (52) G major
                Organ: Queen's Hall, London
                His Master's Voice DB 1402, 78 r.p.m.
                Victor 7271, 78 r.p.m.
    (53) A minor
        a)   Decca DK 1949, 78 r.p.m.
        b)   See No. 49

Presto, from Sonata I, BWV 525
                See No. 24

*L'Association des Amis de l'Art de Marcel Dupré, 21 Boulevard Exelmans, 75016, Paris.

55   Sinfonia, from Cantata XXIX ("We thank Thee, O God") (arr. Dupré)
         His Master's Voice DB 4002, 78 r.p.m.

56   Toccata in D minor ("Dorian"), BWV 538
         See No. 35a

57   Toccata, Adagio and Fugue in C major, BWV 564
         Decca AR 14278-83, 78 r.p.m.

58-60   Toccatas and Fugues
     (58) D minor, BWV 565
         Organ: Saint-Sulpice, Paris
         Lumen 3.26.012, 78 r.p.m.
     (59) D minor ("Dorian"), BWV 538
         See No. 29
     (60) F major, BWV 540
         See No. 29

Works of Clérambault

61   *Basse et Dessus de Trompette*
         Organ: Queen's Hall, London
         His Master's Voice DB 1137, 78 r.p.m.

Works of Couperin

62   Mass: *Usage des Couvents, L'*
         Collector's Series
         Westminster 9351

Works of Daquin

63   *Coucou, Le*
         See No. 1

64   *Noël*
         See No. 61

Works of Franck

65   Chorales: E major, B minor, A minor
     a)   Decca (E) 3090/91 — (B) 2188/89 — (A) 1859/60, 78 r.p.m.
     b)   Organ: St. Thomas, New York
         Mercury MG 50168, SR 90168

66-67   Fantasies
     (66) C major
          a)   Decca LM 4513, 10 in.
                    London LS-137, 10 in.
          b)   See No. 51c
     (67) A major

                    Dupré à Saint-Sulpice, Vol. III
                    Olympian Series
                    Mercury MG 50228, SR 90228

68   *Grande Pièce Symphonique*
                    See No. 67

69   *Pastorale*
          a)   Organ: Queen's Hall, London
                    His Master's Voice D1145, 78 r.p.m.
                    Disque Gramophone W793, 78 r.p.m.
          b)   See No. 67

70   Pièce Héroïque
          a)   Organ: Queen's Hall, London
                    His Master's Voice D1115, 78 r.p.m.
                    Disque Gramophone W757, 78 r.p.m.
                    Victor 9121, 78 r.p.m
          b)   See No. 65b

71   Prelude, Fugue and Variation
                    Organ: Queen's Hall London
                    His Master's Voice D1843, 78 r.p.m.
                    Disque Gramophone W1165, 78 r.p.m.

Works of Frescobaldi

72   Toccata

                    Organ: Dupré residence, Meudon
                    L'Anthologie Sonore 4, 78 r.p.m.
                    Haydn Society AS-11

Works of Gabrieli

73   Ricercar for four voices
                    See No. 72

Works of Handel

74   Concerto in B-flat, op. 4, no. 2, for organ and orchestra (arr. for organ solo by Dupré)
                    His Master's Voice DB 5045, 78 r.p.m.

75   Concerto in D minor for organ and orchestra (arr. for organ solo by
      Dupré)
                        See No. 51c

Works of Mendelssohn

76   Finale, from Sonata I in F minor
                        See No. 24

77   Sonata IV in B-flat
                        Organ: Queen's Hall, London
                        His Master's Voice D1433, 78 r.p.m.
                        His Master's Voice E438, 10 in., 78 r.p.m.
                        Disque Gramophone W1211, 78 r.p.m.
                        Disque Gramophone P1011, 10 in., 78 r.p.m.

Works of Messiaen

78   *Banquet céleste, Le*
                        See 16a

79   *Bergers Les,* from *La Nativité du Seigneur*
                        See No. 16a

Works of Mozart

80-81 Fantasies
       (80) F minor, K. 594
                        Organ: Saint-Sulpice, Paris
                        Overtone OV 14
                        Lumen LD 2.112
       (81) F minor, K.608
                        See No. 80

82   Fugue in C minor (arr. Dupré)
                        Organ: Queen's Hall, London
                        His Master's Voice DB 4002, 78 r.p.m.

Works of Pachelbel

83   Chorale Prelude: *Our Father who art in heaven*
                        Organ: Dupré residence, Meudon
                        L'Anthologie Sonore 10, 78 r.p.m.
                        Haydn Society AS-11

Works of Saint-Saëns

84   *Cygne, Le* (arr. Dupré)
                Organ: Queen's Hall, London
                His Master's Voice E 518, 10 in., 78 r.p.m.
                Disque Gramophone P 789, 10 in., 78 r.p.m.
                Victor 1430, 10 in., 78 r.p.m.

85   Prelude in E-flat
                See No. 84

86   Symphony III in C minor, op. 78 (with Paul Paray conducting the Detroit Symphony Orchestra)
                Olympian Series
                Organ: Ford Auditorium, Detroit
                Mercury MG 50167, SR 90012

Works of Scheidt

87   Chorale Prelude: *We all believe in one God*
                See No. 83

Works of Widor

88   Allegro, from Sixth Symphony
          a)   Organ: Alexandra Palace, London
                His Master's Voice D 1942, 78 r.p.m.
          b)   See No. 18c

89   *Salve Regina*
                See No. 18c

90-92 Symphonies
     (90) Fifth in F minor
                Organ: Saint-Sulpice, Paris
                Westminster XWN 18871, WST 14871
     (91) Ninth in C minor ("Gothic")
                See No. 90
     (92) Variations, from Fifth Symphony
                Organ: Alexandra Palace, London
                His Master's Voice D1898, 78 r.p.m.

Appendix F

BOOKS ABOUT DUPRÉ

Delestre, Abbé R. *L'Œuvre de Marcel Dupré*. Paris: Éditions Musique Sacrée, 1952.

An admirable work which traces principal stages in Dupré's life and which provides brief analyses of his compositions. Published in 1952, it does not discuss the last nineteen years of his career and artistic production.

Gavoty, Bernard. *Marcel Dupré*. "Les Grands Intérprètes." Geneva: Éditions René Kister, 1955.

A brief portrait of Marcel Dupré drawn with several "real-life" stories. Roger Hauert's photography is excellent. F. E. Richardson's English translation was published by Éditions René Kister in 1957.

ACKNOWLEDGMENTS

FRITZ BERNHARD, Zurich: Figures 11, 37 and 50
MICHAEL BRODSKY, Paris: Figure 35
NELSON E. BUECHNER, Philadelphia: Figure 33
DURAND et CIE., Paris: Figures 13 and 38. Used by permission of the publisher. Elkan-Vogel, Inc. sole representative U.S.A.
ELLEBÉ, Rouen: Figures 4 and 6
G. FELICI, Rome: Figure 44
W. H. HOLDT STUDIOS, INC., Philadelphia: Figure 34
Madame H. HUMBRECHT, Paris: Figure 16
LOCHEROY, Paris: Figure 48
LESTER OAKES, Blairstown: Figure 45
ROGER PERRIN, Paris: Figure 36
JOHN RODGERS, New York: Figure 47 and Back Cover
H. ROGER VIOLLET, Paris: Figures 24 and 39
All other photographs and documents are from the Dupré family archives.

INDEX OF PERSONS CITED